PRACTICING
EDIFICATION
IN UTTERANCE
Exploring Paul's Instructions to Corinth

S. SEKOU ABODUNRIN

Practicing Edification in Utterance
Exploring Paul's instructions to Corinth

Sekou Publishing

sekou@sekou.me

Copyright © 2021 by Sekou Abodunrin

All designs by
Kenteba Kreations
contact.kenteba@gmail.com

ISBN: 978-1-912921-05-8
Published by Sekou Publishing. All rights reserved.

Unless otherwise indicated, all Scripture quotations are taken from the King James Version of the Bible.

Some Scripture quotations marked (AMPC) are taken from Amplified Bible, Classic Edition (AMPC) Copyright © 1954, 1958, 1962, 1964, 1965, 1987 by The Lockman Foundation.

Some Scripture quotations marked (AMPLIFIED) are taken from Amplified Bible, Copyright © 2015 by The Lockman Foundation, La Habra, CA 90631. All rights reserved.

Some Scripture quotations marked (CEV) are taken from Contemporary English Version (CEV), Copyright © 1995 by American Bible Society;

Some Scripture quotations marked (TPT) are taken from The Passion Translation®. Copyright © 2017, 2018, 2020 by Passion & Fire Ministries, Inc. Used by permission. All rights reserved. thePassionTranslation.com

Scripture quotations marked (NIV) are taken from THE HOLY BIBLE, NEW INTERNATIONAL VERSION®. Copyright© 1973, 1978, 1984,

In scripture quotes, the author has rendered words in italics in bold CAPITALS to make it easier for the reader to spot these.

In scripture quotes, the author has rendered words in italics in bold CAPITALS to make it easier for the reader to spot these.

TABLE OF CONTENTS

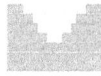

INTRODUCTION

As students of God's word, we must remain vulnerable enough that it dissolve our haziness on matters of doctrine. We make it our aim to submit our minds to the power of God's word so it becomes our practice.

After hearing the saints speaking in tongues in Acts 2, the religious crowd at Jerusalem were amazed and in doubt saying "what meaneth this". The audience of Peter's day quickly reached a wrong conclusion, that "these men are full of new wine". Apparently, people do not understand utterance just by listening to what was said or observing its practice.

Responding, Peter explained, "these are not drunken as you suppose". He grounds them in the words of the prophets, which Jesus had taught to him for 40 days post-resurrection. Although Peter had a phenomenal ministry in bringing men to an understanding of utterance, and was the spokesman in Acts 2, the Lord did not use Peter to document his rich understanding. This task was given to Paul.

Therefore, Paul's writings in 1 Corinthians 12, 13 and 14 are worthy of our study as student of the scriptures. If we are going to benefit from the apostolic instructions in 1 Corinthians, we must realize that by putting it in the scriptures, the Spirit is making a point. Since Peter freely admits to reading all of Paul's epistles, then, Peter read the letter to Corinth and was blessed by its contents. Evidently, the Spirit wants us to address that which is Corinthian in our thinking or practice.

There is a tendency to approach the 1 Corinthians 14 text in fragments. However, approaching the text that way leaves us with fragmented understanding of the Apostle's mind. However, as we study these chapters together, we trust that we will better understand and practice the scriptures. We are all Corinthians following the apostles as we sail with the Corinthians and navigating our way through apostolic scripture.

Utterance should not be mysterious; however, it is every so often treated as beyond the understanding of the saints. Speaking in tongues is good. Even better is doing so from a sound foundation in the truth of God's word, for in the final analysis, our worship of God is in our understanding of His word. Therefore, our practice must be rooted in God's word.

There are always questions on people's minds regarding the subject of utterance in general and tongues in particular. As ministers, we must encourage these questions and readily answer them from the Bible. The teacher who keeps tackling these questions by getting clearer in explanation is an asset to the saints of the Bible. The saints get edified as confusion gives way to clarity and persuasion.

While I taught a series in the spring of 2021, many listeners requested the teachings in book form. While this book does not cover the full scope of that series, it addresses portions from our treatment of 1 Corinthians 12, 13 and 14.

NB – In scripture quotes, the author has rendered words in italics in bold CAPITALS to make it easier for the reader to spot these.

Kent 2021

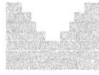

ACKNOWLEDGEMENT

This book is dedicated to the tireless students of His Word who crave an understanding of the practice of utterance and edification in the local church.

To Olatee and the saints at GracePlace who have been so patient with me through the years and especially as I taught a body of knowledge much wider than that covered in this book night after night through the COVID lockdown of the Spring of 2020 through the Spring of 2021.

Thank you.

1

I WOULD NOT HAVE YOU IGNORANT

> 1. Now concerning spiritual **GIFTS**, brethren, I would not have you ignorant.
> 1 Corinthians 12:1

Paul identified the key problem of the Corinthians – they were ignorant. The word translated "ignorant" is from two Greek words "**a**" (a negative particle) and "**noeo**" (to apply mental effort needed to reach bottom-line conclusions, to consider, to think, to be intelligent, or to be informed). Thus, the word carries the idea to willfully ignore. It is a deliberate action, a refusal to apply the mental effort needed to reach correct conclusions.

This was an ignorance of a knowledge already possessed (for example, what Paul had taught them orally or the letters that Paul had written to them).

What was Paul's response to their ignorance? He said, "I give you to understand". This is better understood as "I make known to you" or "I inform you" (see 1 Corinthians 12:3). Paul did not tell them to just do whatever comes to them. They needed to understand.

The saints understand by reading:

4. Whereby, when ye read, ye may understand my knowledge in

the mystery of Christ)
Ephesians 3:4

The word translated "when ye read" is from two Greek words that mean "to be sure again", "to recognize again", or "to know again". It means to know accurately to be able to distinguish between things. This is being thorough.

Thus, the saints will know by reading thoroughly.

What were they to read? They were to read "my knowledge in the mystery of Christ". Paul had written down apostolic knowledge for the saints to thoroughly read so they could distinguish between things.

However, though Paul had taught the Corinthians, they were not thoroughly reading his writings and began to ignore things that they should not have. Consequently, their practice of spiritual things became shabby.

The nature of the Corinthian ignorance

Paul's "I would not have you ignorant" shows that even in the matter of spirituals, the believer is first a disciple of the written word. The disciple improves his administration of spirituals by increasing his word in-take.

Furthermore, a student of the word would observe that Paul is big on knowledge in Corinth:

16. Know ye not that ye are the temple of God, and **THAT** the Spirit of God dwelleth in you?
1 Corinthians 3:16

It was not enough for the Corinthians to be the temple of the Spirit in the new creation – they were also to be students of that knowledge.

2. Do ye not know that the saints shall judge the world? and if
the world shall be judged by you, are ye unworthy to judge the
smallest matters?
1 Corinthians 6:2

Paul knew that if they gave their minds to the knowledge that
the saints will judge the world, it would radically change their
behaviour towards each other.

3. Know ye not that we shall judge angels? how much more
things that pertain to this life?
1 Corinthians 6:3

Again, he wanted them to know that the saints shall judge angels. He knew that this knowledge would affect how they con-
ducted their affairs in the natural.

15. Know ye not that your bodies are the members of Christ?
shall I then take the members of Christ, and make **THEM** the
members of an harlot? God forbid. 16. What? know ye not
that he which is joined to an harlot is one body? for two, saith
he, shall be one flesh.
1 Corinthians 6:15-16

Observe the double "Know ye not".

Paul was correcting his audience regarding the 1 Corinthians 5
issue by reminding them about the knowledge that they were to
give their minds to. The Corinthians had been naughty because
they had not paid attention to the right knowledge.

The "he" in "for two, saith he" refers to Moses' writings in Genesis 2:24. What Paul did not want these Corinthians to ignore
was the proper understanding of the writings of Moses, the
prophets, and the psalms.

> 1. Moreover, brethren, I would not that ye should be ignorant,
> how that all our fathers were under the cloud, and all passed
> through the sea;
> 1 Corinthians 10:1

The "I would not that" is not a mere wish.

The very things Paul did not want these Corinthians to ignore were the writings of Moses in the Holy scriptures thousands of years before. But these saints had become sloppy spiritually because they had not thoroughly read the Holy scriptures. Although they had seen how to read them in the examples given by the apostles, the Corinthians had simply ignored it.

The expression "I would not that ye should be ignorant" is then repeated in 1 Corinthian 12:1.

> 1. Now concerning spiritual **GIFTS**, brethren, I would not
> have you ignorant.
> 1 Corinthians 12:1

We must realise that "I would not" is not a mere wish, evident in the apostle dedicating three entire chapters to teach along these lines. How many issues were so important that any of the apostles dedicated three continuous chapters to in all of God's word? Paul is not merely expressing a wish. "I would not" is a grave word. It is to be understood as "it is not allowed", or "not permissible".

The "Ye" in "I would not that ye should be ignorant" is an old English plural pronoun meaning "all of you". So Paul's "I would not that ye should be ignorant" meant that you would never find a believer that ignorance looks good on.

Paul's emphasis on instructions about knowledge shows that revelation knowledge plays a very large role in the life of the saint.

Why then was it so easy for the saints at Corinth to ignore the apostolic knowledge?

> 1. Now concerning spiritual gifts, brethren, I would not have you ignorant. 2. Ye know that ye were Gentiles, carried away unto these dumb idols, even as ye were led.
>
> 1 Corinthians 12:1-2

The word translated "you know" in verse 2, means "to turn the attention to something", "to notice", or "to cherish in the heart". Paul said this concerning his use of spirituals in the previous verse where he had said "Now concerning spiritual gifts…". Also, the word translated "spiritual" is the word **pneumatikos**, meaning "that which is in the spirit", "of the spirit" or "has to do with the spirit".

As gentiles, the Corinthians were familiar with the word "**pneumatikos**", but their understanding would have been from their pagan culture and not from the gospel. So they ignored Paul's **pneumatikos** from the gospel and held on to their pagan understanding of spirits. Their prioritization of non-gospel knowledge over the apostolic instructions on spirituals resulted to their erratic thinking and practice.

The saints at Corinth were ignorant because they chose not to receive Paul's instructions, discarding the knowledge of **pneumatikos** from the gospel. They were still thinking in terms of "these dumb idols, even as ye were led".

So, when Paul says, "concerning spiritual gifts, brethren, I would not have you ignorant", he was saying that he did not want them to continue without engaging their minds. He did not mean that they were without knowledge. Rather, he meant they were not engaging or prioritizing that mind or knowledge of **pneumatikos** that he had delivered to them. Unlearning the old ways of thinking was tough.

Understand Paul's spiritual

What had Paul told them?

> 11. If we have sown unto you spiritual things, **IS IT** a great
> thing if we shall reap your carnal things?
> 1 Corinthians 9:11

The word translated "spiritual" is the same word **pneumatikos** that was later used in 1 Corinthians 12:1. Also, the original Greek text only reads "spirituals" not "spiritual things".

Since Paul said "we have sown unto you", he includes himself in the "we". In verse 1, he had said, "Am I not an apostle?". Thus, "we have sown" does not describe agriculture but Paul's apostolic ministry.

> 1. Paul, a servant of Jesus Christ, called **TO BE** an apostle,
> separated unto the gospel of God,
> Romans 1:1

Paul had described his ministry as his being separated unto the gospel of God. Thus, it was as an apostle who ministered the gospel of God that Paul had sown or planted spirituals. Since the "spiritual" that Paul sowed is the gospel of God, then the statement "we have sown unto you spiritual things" can be read as "we have taught you the gospel".

Thus, the saint who has been taught the gospel has been taught "spirituals". The believer's correct understanding of spirituals is to be in the knowledge of the gospel.

> 2. This only would I learn of you, Received ye the Spirit by the
> works of the law, or by the hearing of faith?
> Galatians 3:2

The spirit is received by the hearing of faith, which is the hearing of the gospel. This "faith" is the faithfulness of God. It is what God has done.

Since the gospel is how the correct knowledge of spirits is communicated, then the hearing of the gospel is the hearing of those things of the spirit. These would be the things that God had done concerning the giving of the spirit.

"Now concerning spiritual gifts" in 1 Corinthians 12:1 would be concerning the understanding of spirits that have been communicated in, by, or through the gospel which we have believed.

Thus, the saint hears the gospel as the things of the spirit, believes those things of the spirit spoken in the preaching of the gospel, and as a result receives the spirit by the gospel. It is this spirit which each Corinthian saint had received by believing the gospel that Paul writes about:

The same spirit

8. For to one is given by the Spirit the word of wisdom; to another the word of knowledge by the same Spirit; 9. To another faith by the same Spirit; to another the gifts of healing by the same Spirit; 10. To another the working of miracles; to another prophecy; to another discerning of spirits; to another **DIVERS** kinds of tongues; to another the interpretation of tongues:
1 Corinthians 12:8-10

Here, Paul showed that the spirit which each Corinthian saint receives by believing the gospel also gives the word of wisdom, the word of knowledge, faith, gifts of healing, the working of miracles, prophecy, discerning of spirits, divers kinds of tongues, and the interpretation of tongues.

Paul's emphasizes a key point repeating "by the same Spirit".

This phrase "By the same spirit" means that the word of knowledge is not from one spirit and the word of wisdom from another. Likewise, the gifts of healing is not from a different spirit from the discerning of spirits, divers kinds of tongues, or the interpretation of tongues. They are all "by the same spirit".

Whereas the pagan has a god dedicated to each special power, in the gospel, we learn that all demonstration of the spirit is from the one spirit received in redemption. It is "by the same spirit". This knowledge that "it is the same spirit" is often ignored.

It is only by the gospel that we come to know of the abilities in the spirit already given by the same gospel and received by believing its message. The thing to note is that the gospel gives the spirit and within that spirit, there are things given to us.

10. To another the working of miracles; to another prophecy; to another discerning of spirits; to another **DIVERS** kinds of tongues; to another the interpretation of tongues:
1 Corinthians 12:10

The spirit given by the gospel is given in the resurrection of Jesus.

Before Jesus' resurrection, in the Genesis through Malachi text, we do not see diverse kinds of tongues and the interpretation of tongues. Though the seven other gifts were displayed at different times, no man had the diversities of tongues and its interpretation before the resurrection of Jesus.

Thus, in the gospel, we see that the distinction in the spirit after the resurrection of Jesus was the diversities of tongues and its interpretation. The resurrection is synonymous with tongues and its interpretation.

When one hears of Paul's **pneumatikos** but thinks with the pagan mindset of the Corinthians, it is easy to think that God demands a separate spirit and diverse sets of qualifications for each of the word of wisdom, the word of knowledge, faith, gifts of healing, the working of miracles, prophecy, discerning of spirits, divers kinds of tongues and the interpretation of tongues. However, such reasoning is not found in the gospel.

The person that ignores the teaching of the apostles by the gospel would say, "I have the spirit, now I need to add tongues to that spirit and after that, I need to go looking for interpretation of tongues".

That is not the gospel way of thinking. Paul would reply, "concerning spiritual gifts, brethren, I would not have you ignorant". The gospel gives the spirit and, in the spirit, all else is given. It is the same spirit.

Tongues as the language of the family of God

10. To another the working of miracles; to another prophecy; to another discerning of spirits; to another **DIVERS** kinds of tongues; to another the interpretation of tongues:
1 Corinthians 12:10

> **Tongues is the family language by the spirit of God.**

In the KJV, the word "divers" in "divers kinds" is italicized. This means that it was added by the translators. In fact, in the original Greek, "diverse kinds" is not two words but one – **genos** – meaning "kinds". It means the aggregate of many individuals of the same nature, kind, sort, or species. It could also mean "countryman", "of a particular nation", "of a family", or "of a tribe or a people".

Diverse kinds of tongues therefore is the tongue of a particular people, a specific nation, or a particular family. This would be the people, nation, or family taught by the gospel.

> 9. But ye **ARE** a chosen generation, a royal priesthood, an holy nation, a peculiar people; that ye should shew forth the praises of him who hath called you out of darkness into his marvellous light:
> 1 Peter 2:9

The Greek word translated "generation" in "chosen genera-tion" is **genos**. This is the word translated "kinds" in "kinds of tongues" in 1 Corinthians 12:10.

The gospel is the call out of the darkness into marvelous light.

Those who have believed the gospel are called a holy or distinct nation. Peter teaches that all that are in this nation by the gospel are holy.

> *Tongues does not happen by itself but worked through the will of the saint.*

That Greek word translated as "holy" means distinct or separate. It is that which is sacred, not gen-eral. The chosen generation are the sacred people or nation of God. Thus, a man is either of the nation of the gospel or the nation that is not in the gospel.

Peter further teaches that the nation that is not in the gospel is "darkness", while the nation in the gospel is called "marvellous light". So, the man that has received the gospel has received membership in a distinct nation by the working of God.

Thus, the saints are called the household or family of faith, be-cause this family is made up of those who have believed the gospel. (See Galatians 6:10).

10. To another the working of miracles; to another prophecy;
to another discerning of spirits; to another **DIVERS** kinds of
tongues; to another the interpretation of tongues:
1 Corinthians 12:10

Given that the correct term is kinds of tongues and that kinds
mean, "of a particular nation", "about a family", "of a tribe"
or "a people", diverse kinds of tongues would be the tongue
of a particular family, which we have shown is elsewhere identified as peculiar people, household of faith, or the household of
God. It is the tongue associated with a distinct people whose
faith in the resurrection differentiates them from all others.

14. For if I pray in an **UNKNOWN** tongue, my spirit prayeth,
but my understanding is unfruitful.
1 Corinthians 14:14 - KJV

Since kinds of tongues is by the
spirit, it means that it is the spirit
received in the gospel that gives the
tongue that is distinct to the family
of God. Hence Paul says, "For if I
pray in an unknown tongue, my spirit prayeth, but my understanding is
unfruitful" (1 Corinthians 14:14).

> *Tongues are*
> *aimed at God, but*
> *interpretation is*
> *directed at the minds*
> *of men.*

Thus, there are vocal abilities that
go with the indwelling of the spirit.
Tongues announce that the speaker
of tongues is of a particular nation or family of men and wom-
en who has been raised with Christ.

Thus, Paul does not explain kinds of tongues as some Pentecos-
tal experience or phenomena.

Tongues is the family language by the spirit of God.

Thus, tongues cannot be spoken by just anyone but those that belong to the family of God.

Importantly, since tongues is the family language by the spirit of God, it is unlike any of the natural languages spoken by the tribes and nations of this earth, for "kinds of tongues" is not learned or acquired by sitting through classes in phonetics. Rather, "kinds of tongues" is the vocal ability of the indwelling spirit given expression through words. It is a resurrection-of-Jesus sound.

Therefore, the expression "kinds of tongues" means that the only kind of tongues that Paul informed the church about is that which the spirit of Christ gives. "Kinds of tongues" does not mean that one saint has one type of tongues and another saint has another type.

If you pay close attention, it is obvious that these "kinds of tongues" would sound different in individual saints.

When investigating "kinds of tongues", we do not use phonetic sounds or change in phonetics to identify, judge, or classify tongues.

The fact that "kinds of tongues" sounds different in the mouth of different saints must not cloud the fact that there is only one gospel. In this gospel, only one spirit is given because there is only one family of God. Since all saints have this same spirit who gives the same vocal ability spoken as tongues, there is only one tongue given irrespective of how it sounds.

So, your tongues sounding different from mine does not mean our tongues are different. They sound different because we each vocalize differently. However, the spirit-given ability is the same.

We classify "kind of tongues" by the source. Since what each of us says is by the indwelling spirit, then my tongue and yours are the same. Only how we say it differs.

> 11. But all these worketh that one and the selfsame Spirit,
> dividing to every man severally as he will.
> 1 Corinthians 12:11

The expression "all these" refers to the gifts in the spirit - the word of wisdom, the word of knowledge, faith, gifts of healing, the working of miracles, prophecy, discerning of spirits, divers kinds of tongues, and the interpretation of tongues, which had been listed in verses 8-10.

Observe that although the list that Paul gives is long, it is that "one and the selfsame Spirit". So do not be fazed by how many demonstrations of the spirit there are. Instead, put your confidence in the "one and the selfsame Spirit".

Also, pay attention to the phrase "dividing to every man severally". The dividing is not apart from men, but it is in men, expressed through men to men among men.

You are that spirit-indwelt man through whom the things in that spirit are divided to men in service.

Paul taught that these things that the spirit gives are worked by the spirit through the will of the spirit indwell man. He meant that others would enjoy what you are given by the spirit through your willingness to express.

What Paul said about the will

Concerning the things of the spirit and the will, Paul continues:

14. For if I pray in an **UNKNOWN** tongue, my spirit prayeth,

but my understanding is unfruitful. 15. What is it then? I will pray with the spirit, and I will pray with the understanding also: I will sing with the spirit, and I will sing with the understanding also.

1 Corinthians 14:14-15

Paul taught the Corinthians "I will pray with the spirit".

He also taught the Corinthians "I will sing with the spirit".

"I will pray" and "I will sing" mean that speaking, praying, or singing in tongues is under your administration. If you are not willing, the audience enjoys nothing because there is nothing spoken by the spirit-indwelt man. Such a man does not need a stronger spirit but a willingness. Whether singing in the spirit or praying in the spirit, it is the will of man that expresses the indwelling spirit of God.

Thus, in Paul's **pneumatikos**, the will that Paul refers to is the will of the man, who by the act of speaking expresses the spirit. Therefore, "kind of tongues" is of the spirit but it is to be worked through the will of the saint. Tongues does not happen by itself.

There is no scarcity in the giving on the part of the spirit because spirit gives to all. Rather, the scarcity is in the working. In other words, "will the man be ready for the working or not by being willing or not".

1. Now concerning spiritual **GIFTS**, brethren, I would not have you ignorant. 2. Ye know that ye were Gentiles, carried away unto these dumb idols, even as ye were led.

1 Corinthians 12:1-2

Again, when Paul says "I would not have you ignorant", he was teaching that the saints were not giving their minds to the proper exercise of the distinct vocal ability that we have in the

indwelling spirit. We give our minds to the fact that the giver
of the gifts is in us so that we recognise our responsibility to
exercise it to edify others.

> 37. If any man think himself to be a prophet, or spiritual, let
> him acknowledge that the things that I write unto you are the
> commandments of the Lord. 38. But if any man be ignorant,
> let him be ignorant.
>
> 1 Corinthians 14:37-38

The Greek word translated spiritual in "a prophet, or spiritual"
is the same one that has been translated "spiritual" in "concerning spiritual gifts, brethren, I would not have you ignorant" in 1
Corinthians 12:1.

The **pneumatikos** (prophet or spiritual) see Paul's writings as
the commandments of the Lord, while the saint not given to
such a perspective sees Paul's writing as communicating a piece
of knowledge on par with the pagan knowledge concerning
spirits.

Paul's "if any man be ignorant" means that after all the apostolic
instructions, which are the Lord's instructions in 1 Corinthians
12, 13, and 14, there are those saints that still ignore these instructions. This "ignorant" in "if any man be ignorant" means
not allowing the knowledge to stay in the mind long enough to
become practice. Paul is instructing the saints not to follow the
practice of ignoring apostolic commands regarding utterance.

"Let him be ignorant" means that the men who ignore what
Paul has written are to be ignored. Paul aims to get every saint
to move from verse 38 to verse 37.

Paul aims to get every saint to move from verse 38 to verse 37.

Where do tongues and its interpretation come from?

8. For to one is given by the Spirit the word of wisdom; to
another the word of knowledge by the same Spirit; 9. To
another faith by the same Spirit; to another the gifts of healing
by the same Spirit; 10. To another the working of miracles; to
another prophecy; to another discerning of spirits; to another
DIVERS kinds of tongues; to another the interpretation of
tongues: 11. But all these worketh that one and the selfsame
Spirit, dividing to every man severally as he will.
1 Corinthians 12:8-11

It is the same indwelling spirit that gives kinds of tongues and
the interpretation of tongues. It is not one spirit who gives
kinds of tongues, while another spirit gives the interpretation
of tongues.

Although tongues and its interpretation are not the same thing,
these two expressions are the same ability by the same spirit.

Interpretation of tongues exists because what is said in tongues
is not directed at men's minds.

Tongues are aimed at God, but interpretation is directed at the
minds of men.

2

IN THE LAW IT IS WRITTEN

Mark records one of Jesus' last face-to-face teachings:

15. And he said unto them, Go ye into all the world, and preach the gospel to every creature. 16. He that believeth and is baptized shall be saved; but he that believeth not shall be damned. 17. And these signs shall follow them that believe; In my name shall they cast out devils; they shall speak with new tongues;

Mark 16:15-17

Jesus taught these words to His disciples after His resurrection.

Jesus said, "they will speak in new tongues".

Who did Jesus say would speak in new tongues? The one that believes the gospel will speak in new tongues.

Jesus taught that new tongues were a sign of the gospel.

> 45. Then opened he their understanding, that they might
> understand the scriptures,
> Luke 24:45

Luke also narrates that after His resurrection, Jesus taught His disciples the scriptures.

> 2. Until the day in which he was taken up, after that he through the Holy Ghost had given commandments unto the apostles whom he had chosen: 3. To whom also he shewed himself alive after his passion by many infallible proofs, being seen of them forty days, and speaking of the things pertaining to the kingdom of God:
> Acts 1:2-3

> *Jesus told us to speak in tongues because that is what He does in the believer.*

Here, Luke shows that after rising from the dead, Jesus taught His disciples for 40 days. It was during this 40-day period that He taught his disciples that they that believed the gospel "shall speak with new tongues in my name".

In Middle Eastern thinking, the name of a person is a measure of his or her accomplishment or worth. Thus, when Jesus said, "In my name", He means in or because of His accomplishment.

> 44. And he said unto them, These **ARE** the words which I spake unto you, while I was yet with you, that all things must be fulfilled, which were written in the law of Moses, and **IN** the prophets, and **IN** the psalms, concerning me. 45. Then opened he their understanding, that they might understand the scriptures, 46. And said unto them, Thus it is written, and thus it behoved Christ to suffer, and to rise from the dead the third day: 47. And that repentance and remission of sins should be preached in his name among all nations, beginning

at Jerusalem.
Luke 24:44-47

Jesus taught the disciples and opened their understanding by showing them that the law of Moses, the prophets and the psalms were concerning Him.

> *Christ gives both the kinds of tongues and the interpretation of tongues by His spirit in His saints.*

After this, He taught them to preach "repentance and remission of sins should be preached in his name". As those He had taught the gospel to preach to people what He had taught them, their hearers would repent (change their minds) and receive remission of sins.

He breathed on them

22. And when he had said this, he breathed on **THEM**, and saith unto them, Receive ye the Holy Ghost: 23. Whose soever sins ye remit, they are remitted unto them; **AND** whose soever **SINS** ye retain, they are retained.
John 20:22-23

What does Jesus mean by "Whose soever sins ye remit, they are remitted unto them"?

It is the Lord that gives remission of sins.

The disciples co-labour with the Lord by preaching to people what Jesus had taught them from the law of Moses, the Prophets, and the Psalms concerning Him. This is how the disciples remit people's sins. People received the Lord's provision of remission of sins by believing the disciples as they preached the gospel.

We can compare Luke and John's accounts:

> **Tongues become God's distinguishing mark of those that have believed in God's provision of rest.**

Luke narrated that Jesus taught extensively from the law of Moses, the prophets, and the psalms concerning Him before He told them to preach "repentance and remission of sins" in His name.

Likewise, John's account says "he breathed on them, and saith unto them, Receive ye the Holy Ghost" before He told them to preach the remission of sins. This is John's way of saying that Jesus taught extensively from the law of Moses, the prophets, and the psalms concerning Himself.

To breathe on them is not referring to passing out of Carbon Dioxide after breathing in oxygen. Rather, to breathe on the disciples is a figure of speech for teaching them the law of Moses, the prophets, and the psalms concerning Himself.

The Greek word translated "receive" in "He breathed on them, and saith unto them, Receive ye the Holy Ghost" is **lambano**, which means to seize or take the Holy Ghost. Given that **lambano** came after He breathed or preached to them, this was Jesus teaching the man who has already believed to receive the remission of sins to act on the knowledge of the indwelling.

Jesus shows that the man who has already believed to receive the remission of sins has received the indwelling of the spirit by believing the gospel. Remission of sins and indwelling are the same thing.

Lambano or receive the spirit is act on what you have in the new birth. They were to take of that spirit which they already had when they believed. Jesus' instruction meant "Do something with the knowledge of the indwelling of the spirit". This is what Jesus taught them for 40 days.

Was Jesus telling them to receive afresh? No.

Were they receiving that which they never had before? No. They were already indwelt by the spirit by believing the gospel.

How did the disciples receive from this indwelling? By doing something - they acted on Jesus' instruction by letting their mouth speak in new tongues in Acts 2:4.

The knowledge of the indwelling spirit as salvation is what a man needs to receive or take hold of the spirit.

Jesus and new tongues

15. And he said unto them, Go ye into all the world, and preach the gospel to every creature. 16. He that believeth and is baptized shall be saved; but he that believeth not shall be damned. 17. And these signs shall follow them that believe; In my name shall they cast out devils; they shall speak with new tongues;
Mark 16:15-17

"In my name they shall speak with new tongues" means that Jesus associates Himself with the man that speaks in tongues because he has believed the gospel.

The scriptures contain numerous accounts of Jesus preaching the gospel and casting out devils – (see Mark 1:14, Matthew 4:23-24, Mark 1:23-27, Luke 4:33-36).

Now, when the believer speaks in tongues, does he or she find the example of speaking in tongues in Christ? This is an important question.

Will Jesus tell His disciples to speak with new tongues if He did not speak in tongues?

> 27. To whom God would make known what **IS** the riches of the glory of this mystery among the Gentiles; which is Christ in you, the hope of glory: 28. Whom we preach, warning every man, and teaching every man in all wisdom; that we may present every man perfect in Christ Jesus:
> Colossians 1:27-28

The riches of the glory of the mystery is Christ in the saint.

Reading verse 27 into verse 28, we see that what we preach is Christ in us. The mystery means that which is to be explained, and this explanation is in the gospel.

> 13. Hereby know we that we dwell in him, and he in us, because he hath given us of his Spirit.
> 1 John 4:13

It is not only true that we entered into Him to dwell in Him, it is also true that He entered into us to dwell in us by giving His Spirit to dwell in us.

> 8. For to one is given by the Spirit the word of wisdom; to another the word of knowledge by the same Spirit; 9. To another faith by the same Spirit; to another the gifts of healing by the same Spirit; 10. To another the working of miracles; to another prophecy; to another discerning of spirits; to another **DIVERS** kinds of tongues; to another the interpretation of tongues: 11. But all these worketh that one and the selfsame Spirit, dividing to every man severally as he will.
> 1 Corinthians 12:8-11

When Paul makes the point that the spirit gives, he is speaking

of Christ giving, for Christ has entered into us to dwell in us by
His spirit which He has given unto us.

We could then say the same spirit that gives kinds of tongues
also gives the interpretation of tongues. Or stated differently,
we could also say that it is the same Christ that gives kinds of
tongues that gives the interpretation of tongues. Christ gives
both the kinds of tongues and the interpretation of tongues by
His spirit in His saints.

Paul described the facts of "the gospel which I preached unto
you" (1 Corinthians 15:1) as "Christ
died for our sins according to the
scriptures and that he was buried,
and that he rose again the third day
according to the scriptures" (see 1
Corinthians 15:3-4). Thus, to believe
the gospel is to believe in the death
burial, and resurrection of Jesus.

> **Tongues show that the speaker is of the household of faith, or the household of God.**

15. And he said unto them, Go ye
into all the world, and preach the
gospel to every creature. 16. He that believeth and is baptized
shall be saved; but he that believeth not shall be damned. 17.
And these signs shall follow them that believe; In my name
shall they cast out devils; they shall speak with new tongues;
Mark 16:15-17

When Jesus says "he that believeth and is baptized shall be
saved", He means he that believes the gospel, which is to believe
the death burial, and resurrection of Jesus. So, the expression
"he that believeth and is baptized shall be saved", is not describing two things but one.

The Greek word **kai** translated as "and" in "he that believeth
and is baptized shall be saved" can either be a connecting word,
or a word that provides further explanation. In this case, Jesus

teaches about salvation by believing the gospel and further explains this believing the gospel as baptism.

This Baptism speaks of a union, where the believer is made one with the Saviour.

Thus, if Jesus tells us that those that believe in the resurrection will speak in new tongues, it is because by believing, we are baptised into Him or made one with Him. Thus, by baptism, we are alive in Him and He is alive in us.

So when the believer preaches the gospel, it is because Jesus is carrying out the gospel task through His saint. When the same believer speaks in new tongues, it is because Jesus is the enablement to speak in tongues.

Jesus told us to speak in tongues because that is what He does in the believer. By supplying tongues by His spirit indwelling His saints, He speaks in tongues.

To understand what speaking in new tongues is, we must realise who these are that Jesus speaks of in "they will speak in new tongues".

There is much that is called "new" in our redemption.

Although we come across Jesus' "you shall speak in new tongues" in Mark's writings, Jesus did not teach that knowledge from reading Mark 16 or from reading any of the writings from Matthew to Revelation. Such writings did not exist in His day.

Jesus is speaking from the Genesis to Malachi text.

New thing, new spirit, new covenant, and new tongues

26. A new heart also will I give you, and a new spirit will I put within you: and I will take away the stony heart out of your flesh, and I will give you an heart of flesh. 27. And I will put my spirit within you, and cause you to walk in my statutes, and ye shall keep my judgments, and do **THEM**.
Ezekiel 36:26-27

"I give you" is God's divine act. His gift by His power.

"I will take away" is God's action.

"Will I put within you" is God's action.

"I will give you an heart of flesh" is that which only God can do.

"I will put my spirit within you". That is God's ability.

God had said that He would give a new heart.

He had said that He would give a new spirit.

He had said, "I will put my spirit within you".

18. Remember ye not the former things, neither consider the things of old. 19. Behold, I will do a new thing; now it shall spring forth; shall ye not know it? I will even make a way in the wilderness, **AND** rivers in the desert.
Isaiah 43:18-19

"Behold" means to see or to look upon.

We are to behold Him.

Isaiah describes God as saying "Behold, I will do a new thing".

Ezekiel had described in great detail that new thing which God does as the giving of a new heart, which is the putting of His spirit into man as a new spirit.

It is by putting His spirit in man that God makes all things new.

Thus, when a man is indwelled by the spirit of God, it will be because God has done the new things that He had said He would do.

God had said through Jeremiah, "I will make a new covenant" (Jeremiah 31:31), which He described as "I will put my law in their inward parts, and write it in their hearts" (Jeremiah 31:33) and He clarified as "I will forgive their iniquity, and I will remember their sin no more" (Jeremiah 31:34).

Thus, what Isaiah calls new thing, Jeremiah calls new covenant, and Ezekiel details as God putting His spirit within man.

Before His crucifixion, Jesus had said:
28. For this is my blood of the new testament, which is shed for many for the remission of sins.
Matthew 26:28

Jesus wants His hearers to hear the fulfilment of Jeremiah's prophesied new testament, which is the blood shed for many for the remission of sins.

The remission of sins is the new thing. Giving a new heart, which is the giving of a new spirit is how God does it. God's new thing is done in Christ.

44. And he said unto them, These **ARE** the words which I spake unto you, while I was yet with you, that all things must be fulfilled, which were written in the law of Moses, and **IN** the prophets, and **IN** the psalms, concerning me.
Luke 24:44

The things that Jesus spoke after His resurrection are not different from those things which Moses, the prophets, and the psalms and even He had spoken of before His sacrifice.

> 15. And he said unto them, Go ye into all the world, and preach the gospel to every creature. 16. He that believeth and is baptized shall be saved; but he that believeth not shall be damned. 17. And these signs shall follow them that believe; In my name shall they cast out devils; they shall speak with new tongues;
> Mark 16:15-17

Therefore, when after His resurrection, Jesus speaks of new tongues, He is not discussing anything other than Isaiah's "new thing", Jeremiah's "new testament", Ezekiel's "new heart", and Ezekiel's "new spirit", which is the new creation.

The "new" in "new tongues" reminds us that the men speaking the tongues are new creation men produced by God who had fulfilled His word.

Who are they, these new creations?

> 9. But ye **ARE** a chosen generation, a royal priesthood, an holy nation, a peculiar people; that ye should shew forth the praises of him who hath called you out of darkness into his marvellous light:
> 1 Peter 2:9

The same Greek word **genos** that had been translated "kinds" in "kinds of tongues" in 1 Corinthians 12:10 has also been translated "generation" in "chosen generation". It is this chosen generation that is called a holy or distinct nation. By producing this new nation of new creation men, God had done the new thing that He promised.

When Jesus teaches concerning "new tongues", we must always recall those things that God had called "new" in the bible.

The "new" in new tongues shows that tongues is a herald that the new things of God have been done.

Paul's writings put Jesus' understanding from the writings of Moses, the prophets, and the psalms into words for the benefit of the saints.

> 21. In the law it is written, With **MEN OF** other tongues and other lips will I speak unto this people; and yet for all that will they not hear me, saith the Lord. 22. Wherefore tongues are for a sign, not to them that believe, but to them that believe not: but prophesying **SERVETH** not for them that believe not, but for them which believe.
> 1 Corinthians 14:21-22

Paul had a universal audience in view

To whom did Paul address these words in 1 Corinthians 14?

> 2. Unto the church of God which is at Corinth, to them that are sanctified in Christ Jesus, called **TO BE** saints, with all that in every place call upon the name of Jesus Christ our Lord, both theirs and ours:
> 1 Corinthians 1:2

Paul wrote "Unto the church of God which is at Corinth with all that in every place call upon the name of Jesus Christ".

To call upon the name of the Lord means to believe the Gospel for salvation (see Romans 10:13). Thus, "all that in every place call upon the name of Jesus Christ" refers to all saints everywhere. This shows that the spirit wants everyone to address that which is "Corinthian" in our thinking or practice.

So, Paul had a universal audience in view.

When Paul gave his phenomenal teaching on utterance to the Corinthians, he was also addressing all the other churches. Thus, when read correctly, the instruction, teaching, and corrections were for all the saints.

Paul had all the saints on his mind in his Corinthian letter.

Right in the middle of his phenomenal teaching on tongues, Paul wrote, "in the law it is written". This shows that his teaching on tongues was not an innovation. He wanted his audience to know that he had not invented the idea of tongues. Rather, his teaching was rooted in the writings of the prophets. He used that teaching to bring his students into the theology of the prophets, who themselves were students of Moses.

Paul expected all students of the scriptures to know that what he had called "kinds of tongues" in 1 Corinthians 12, was not something that the holy scriptures had been silent on. When he said "in the law", he was referring to the sacred text from Genesis through Malachi. Particularly, Paul's 1 Corinthians 14 text explains Isaiah 28. Thus, Paul intended that the saints see the book of Isaiah as a foundation for understanding the purpose of tongues in the local church.

Since Paul said he was "saying none other things than those which the prophets and Moses did say should come" (Acts 26:22), when Paul taught from Isaiah 28, he was not speaking out of context but saying exactly what Isaiah said. Thus, we find that 1 Corinthians 14:21 explains Isaiah 28:11-12.

Corinth via Isaiah

21. In the law it is written, With **MEN OF** other tongues and other lips will I speak unto this people; and yet for all that will

they not hear me, saith the Lord.
1 Corinthians 14:21

The expression, "men of other tongues," is from the Greek word heteroglossos, which means, "speaking languages (tongue) other than one's own." This word is only used here in all of the text from Matthew to Revelation.

The KJV translators correctly italicize "men" in "with men of other tongues and other lips will I speak unto this people". The original text just reads "with other tongues and other lips will I speak unto this people", which is Isaiah 28:11.

> 11. For with stammering lips and another tongue will he speak to this people. 12. To whom he said, This IS the rest **WHEREWITH** ye may cause the weary to rest; and this **IS** the refreshing: yet they would not hear.
> Isaiah 28:11-12

This is Isaiah's text, which Paul explained in 1 Corinthians 14:21.

In the Isaiah text, we find that "stammering lips and another tongue" is to be understood in the context of "this is the rest wherewith ye may cause the weary to rest". The word translated "rest" in "this is the rest wherewith ye may cause the weary to rest" means a resting place or quietness.

Similarly, the writer of Hebrews wrote:

> 3. For we which have believed do enter into rest, as he said, As I have sworn in my wrath, if they shall enter into my rest: although the works were finished from the foundation of the world.
> Hebrews 4:3

When the writer of Hebrews says "as he said", the writer was teaching from Psalm 95:11. The writer of Hebrews taught about rest because the Psalmist had taught it.

The word translated "rest" in "if they shall enter into my rest" in Psalm 95:11 is also translated as "rest" in "this is the rest wherewith ye may cause the weary to rest" in Isaiah 28:12.

This rest is the salvation which is the work of God.

The writer of Hebrews also says:
22. But ye are come unto mount Sion, and unto the city of the living God, the heavenly Jerusalem, and to an innumerable company of angels, 23. To the general assembly and church of the firstborn, which are written in heaven, and to God the Judge of all, and to the spirits of just men made perfect, 24. And to Jesus the mediator of the new covenant, and to the blood of sprinkling, that speaketh better things than **THAT OF** Abel.
Hebrews 12:22-24

Zion is where the church of the firstborn is, the work of Jesus as mediator of the new covenant. This is God's salvation of the believer.

The psalmist says this:
13. For the LORD hath chosen Zion; he hath desired **IT** for his habitation. 14. This **IS** my rest for ever: here will I dwell; for I have desired it.
Psalms 132:13-14

Zion is God's rest forever. God's work of salvation where the work of Jesus the Mediator of the new covenant is rest.

The Hebrew word that has been translated "rest" in "this is my rest for ever" in Psalms 132:14 is also translated as "rest" in "this is the rest wherewith ye may cause the weary to rest" in Isaiah 28:12.

God's rest is where He dwells, and He dwells in us by His spirit. So, salvation is God finding His place of rest in a man who God has made God's habitation. Thus, rest, Zion, and Christ's sacrifice all refer to the same thing.

The psalmist provides God's answer for a question God had posed in Isaiah:

> 1. Thus saith the LORD, The heaven **IS** my throne, and the earth **IS** my footstool: where **IS** the house that ye build unto me? and where **IS** the place of my rest?
> Isaiah 66:1

Now we know God's answer to God's question "where is the place of my rest?

In Psalms 132:13-14, the LORD hath chosen Zion for resting place forever.

We know God's answer to God's question "where is the house that ye build unto me?"

In Psalms 132:13-14, we see that we do not build Him any house. Instead, the LORD choice is Zion, which are the men that He has built as His habitation forever.

God's rest is the refreshing

> 12. To whom he said, This **IS** the rest **WHEREWITH** ye may cause the weary to rest; and this **IS** the refreshing: yet they would not hear.
> Isaiah 28:12

Who is "he" in "to whom he said, this is the rest"? "He" refers to God.

The weary is the man who is weighed down by self-righteousness. Self-righteousness is being without God-given rest. Rest is God's provision. A man finds God's rest to be refreshing.

So salvation is two things at once. On one hand, it is God resting in a man to make that man God's habitation or house. On the other hand, it is man resting in God's labour and ceasing from weariness. This is salvation as man entering into God.

> 16. Therefore thus saith the Lord GOD, Behold, I lay in Zion for a foundation a stone, a tried stone, a precious corner **STONE**, a sure foundation: he that believeth shall not make haste.
> Isaiah 28:16

Here, Isaiah demonstrated that "he that believeth" and "Zion" are the same. Zion is the people of God and not some postcode on earth.

Further, Isaiah showed that the "rest wherewith ye may cause the weary to rest" is the foundation stone that God laid in Zion. He described rest as "he that believeth shall not make haste". In other words, the one that has believed to receive God's rest as His gift to man, will not get into the labour of self-righteousness.

> 11. For with stammering lips and another tongue will he speak to this people. 12. To whom he said, This **IS** the rest **WHEREWITH** ye may cause the weary to rest; and this **IS** the refreshing: yet they would not hear.
> Isaiah 28:11-12

Isaiah spoke of two categories of people. First, there are the weary who would rest and then there are the weary who would not hear. The weary who would not hear is the unbelieving who do not heed God's word. The weary who rest are those who hear and believe God's word.

What did God say to the people? God said "This is the rest wherewith ye may cause the weary to rest". God also said, "this is the refreshing"

What did Isaiah say about the people? Isaiah said, "yet they would not hear".

What was the other thing that these people who would not hear say? They called what was happening "stammering lips"

"Stammering" is not God's description of His gift to men – He calls it rest, which is a refreshing. It is the unbelieving man's evaluation of what God has done in His men. "Stammering lips" is what the weary that will not rest concludes.

The men that believe, which are the men that heed God's provision of rest refer to this as "another tongue".

In the Septuagint, which is the Greek Old Testament (the only Greek translation of the Hebrew scriptures in the time of the apostles) that was quoted by Paul, the word translated "another" in "stammering lips and another tongue" is the word **heteros**, which means another not of the same class or kind.

Since Paul brought up Isaiah 28:11 in his explanation of tongues, this **heteros** tongue refers to the language of those in Zion (from Isaiah 28:16). This corresponds to kinds of tongues, which is the language of a particular family nation or tribe that distinguishes it from all others.

Isaiah 28:11's **heteros** (another of a different type) tongue is the tongues associated with the new covenant in Jesus' sacrifice. This is the language of rest in Zion. This is what Jesus referred to as new tongues.

These texts in Isaiah are the background of Paul's Corinthians text.

Tongues are for a sign

21. In the law it is written, With **MEN OF** other tongues and
other lips will I speak unto this people; and yet for all that will
they not hear me, saith the Lord. 22. Wherefore tongues are
for a sign, not to them that believe, but to them that believe
not: but prophesying **SERVETH** not for them that believe
not, but for them which believe.
1 Corinthians 14:21-22

Paul's conclusion from the Isaiah 28 text is "wherefore tongues
are for a sign". There is a definite article before the word
"tongues" in Greek of this text. Thus, "this tongue" that Isaiah
prophesied about is for a sign.

A sign is a miracle that points away from itself to a message.

We need to understand what the message is.

11. For with stammering lips and another tongue will he
speak to this people. 12. To whom he said, This **IS** the rest
WHEREWITH ye may cause the weary to rest; and this **IS**
the refreshing: yet they would not hear.
Isaiah 28:11-12

We have shown that God was speaking to men of the work of
Christ as rest in Zion.

Which people were these? The men that would not hear. Otherwise, the unbelievers. So, Paul concluded that tongues are a sign
to them that believe not.

What is signified or what does the sign mean? It signifies that
the men who speak in tongues do so to showcase that they have

entered God's provision of rest in Zion. Tongues become God's distinguishing mark of those that have believed in God's provision of rest (the gospel). The man who believes the gospel is of God's holy nation and he speaks in tongues to mark himself as being of the church of God.

Here is what Paul had said in introducing tongues to Corinth:

10. To another the working of miracles; to another prophecy; to another discerning of spirits; to another **DIVERS** kinds of tongues; to another the interpretation of tongues:

1 Corinthians 12:10

The word "divers" is in italics, so it is not there. It is kinds of tongues.

Again, the Greek translated kinds is **genos**, which means countryman, "of a particular nation", "of a particular family", of a tribe or a people. In this case, the people who have believed the gospel. Thus, kinds of tongues is a distinction.

Tongues is the saints' God-given ability, the family language by the spirit of God, which designates the speaker as a believer in the gospel. Tongues show that the speaker is of the household of faith, or the household of God.

By quoting Isaiah, Paul demonstrates that the one speaking in tongues is speaking in another tongue. The Greek for "another" is **heteros**, a word that means not of the same class or kind. It means that those in Zion are a new nation speaking a new tongue as proof of a new covenant. Tongues signify that those men that God has given His spirit have a new language for they are a new nation.

Isaiah's sign to his audience is that in their unbelief, they are not the new nation, therefore they would not understand the tongue of this other nation.

Therefore, tongues is a sign in that the one who has not heeded or believed what God has said about rest in Zion (the gospel) will not speak in tongues. When the man that has believed speaks in tongues, the man who has not believed does not understand. This is a metaphor for the man's unbelief hindering him from receiving and participating in God's new thing – rest in Zion.

3

HE WILL WORSHIP GOD

> **The man who does not believe the gospel will naturally not agree with tongues also.**

21. In the law it is written, With **MEN OF** other tongues and other lips will I speak unto this people; and yet for all that will they not hear me, saith the Lord. 22. Wherefore tongues are for a sign, not to them that believe, but to them that believe not: but prophesying **SERVETH** not for them that believe not, but for them which believe. 23. If therefore the whole church be come together into one place, and all speak with tongues, and there come in **THOSE THAT ARE** unlearned, or unbelievers, will they not say that ye are mad? 24. But if all prophesy, and there come in one that believeth not, or **ONE** unlearned, he is convinced of all, he is judged of all: 25. And thus are the secrets of his heart made manifest; and so falling down on HIS face he will worship God, and report that God is in you of a truth.
1 Corinthians 14:21-25

In the passage above, we see that Paul does not find it absurd that the whole church can speak in tongues, because the church comprises those speaking in tongues. The one coming in and not understanding what is said is the unbeliever. "Will they not say that ye are mad?" is the unbeliever's conclusion.

The man who does not believe the gospel will naturally not agree with tongues also.

We have shown that Paul wrote "in the law it is written" in 1 Corinthians 14:21 he had Isaiah 28:11-12 in view. He was instructing the Corinthians from Isaiah's teaching concerning rest in Zion. Therefore, the expression "will they not say you are mad" is Paul's explanation from Isaiah 28:12

This is the Isaiah text:
12. To whom he said, This **IS** the rest **WHEREWITH** ye may cause the weary to rest; and this **IS** the refreshing: yet they would not hear.
Isaiah 28:12

Paul's "will they not say you are mad?" is from Isaiah's "yet they will not hear".

> *Speaking in tongues is a sign of believing the gospel.*

What would Paul's conclusion be in such a scenario? He would affirm "the whole church has come together into one place". They could do better but they are the church and not the mad ones.

In 1 Corinthians 14:5, where there was the problem of tongues and no interpretation, Paul did not call the speakers mad, but encouraged them to interpret for the edification of those present.

16. Else when thou shalt bless with the spirit, how shall he that occupieth the room of the unlearned say Amen at thy giving of thanks, seeing he understandeth not what thou sayest? 17.

For thou verily givest thanks well, but the other is not edified.
1 Corinthians 14:16-17

Similarly, where there was the problem of giving thanks in
tongues in the hearing of the whole
assembly without interpretation,
Paul did not call those giving thanks
in tongues mad. Rather, he affirmed
them saying, "thou verily givest
thanks well", and encouraged them
to interpret for the edification of
those present.

> **Jesus shows that
> our knowledge
> of God is our
> worship of God.**

Thus, it is the unbeliever that says,
"ye are mad" on account of uninterpreted tongues in the assembly.

Since it is the church that is gathered, we agree with Paul and
identify them as such. "You are the saved" is what the learned
person would have recognized.

Given the apostle's careful wording of the chapter, it is unbelief
that says "ye are mad" in such scenarios.

Thus, when Paul puts the words "you are mad" in the mouths
of the unbelievers, he is unmasking their unbelief in that the
unbelievers reached a conclusion that failed to see what God
had done in His saints. They saw madness, where they should
have seen saints. Here is man referring to God's work as foolish-
ness or madness.

Speaking in tongues is a sign of believing the gospel, while
conclusions about tongues unmask a misunderstanding of the
gospel. Paul wanted the saints to see that the unbelievers' conclusion about the man speaking in tongues mirrors unbelief in
their hearts towards the gospel. "You are mad" shows the extent
of unbelief. It shows that the unbeliever has not received God's

offer of salvation.

The unbeliever observing the saints speak in tongues is observing a sign, for he cannot speak to God in tongues for devotion. He does not understand and cannot participate in such devotion on account of his unbelief. The tongues being spoken judge the unbelief in the unbelievers. The unbeliever does not understand what is being said and continues to conclude that the saints are mad. This hardens unbelief.

If the church continues to speak in tongues without giving words in understanding, the unbeliever would insist on his unbelief, asserting that the speaker in tongues is mad. The unbeliever is not saved of the self-imposed bondage. He would remain in unbelief without a way out.

What should the church do knowing God is not willing that any perish?

9. The Lord is not slack concerning his promise, as some men count slackness; but is longsuffering to us-ward, not willing that any should perish, but that all should come to repentance.
2 Peter 3:9

Since God's long suffering is towards man's salvation, and not their destruction, the church (the speaker in tongues) must co-labour with God to reach the unbelievers.

How does the unbeliever worship God?

24. But if all prophesy, and there come in one that believeth not, or **ONE** unlearned, he is convinced of all, he is judged of all: 25. And thus are the secrets of his heart made manifest; and so falling down on **HIS** face he will worship God, and report that God is in you of a truth.
1 Corinthians 14:24-25

So, the speakers in tongues follow up their speaking in tongues with words spoken in the understanding to the unbelievers. This is prophecy. Here, prophecy is the church's co-labouring with God so the unbeliever can be rescued.

"The secrets of his heart" is the unbelief that is now laid bare.

The unbeliever "will worship God" when the speakers in tongues switch to speaking words in understanding.

> 9. But in vain they do worship me, teaching **FOR** doctrines the commandments of men.
> Matthew 15:9

The word "worship does not only mean and should not be limited only to worship of God in songs. It is more than that. Jesus shows that our knowledge of God is our worship of God. Thus, the poor doctrine is poor worship, while sound doctrine is true worship.

Jesus linked worship to spirit and truth:

> 24. God **IS** a Spirit: and they that worship him must worship **HIM** in spirit and in truth.
> John 4:24

The Greek word for "truth" in the above verse means "reality". So when we speak of spirit we have spoken of worship. Worship of God and spirit are the same thing. A man without the spirit is not in the worship of God.

That means the spirit is the reality of the worship of God.

> 16. And I will pray the Father, and he shall give you another Comforter, that he may abide with you for ever; 17. **EVEN** the Spirit of truth; whom the world cannot receive, because it

seeth him not, neither knoweth him: but ye know him; for he
dwelleth with you, and shall be in you.

John 14:16-17

Jesus also explained that the spirit of truth is the Comforter to
be in us – He had said that this spirit or comforter "shall be in
you".

The indwelling of the spirit is the reality of the worship of God.

> 7. Nevertheless I tell you the truth; It is expedient for you
> that I go away: for if I go not away, the Comforter will not
> come unto you; but if I depart, I will send him unto you. 8.
> And when he is come, he will reprove the world of sin, and
> of righteousness, and of judgment: 9. Of sin, because they
> believe not on me;
>
> John 16:7-9

What does Jesus mean by the Comforter coming unto men?

The Comforter is the spirit of God dwelling in the men that
have believed the gospel.

The Comforter that reproves the world is the spirit living in the
man that believes.

The spirit or Comforter that reproves men, is the spirit that
indwells the man that believes.

Thus, the spirit convicts men of sin (unbelief) by those men
who are indwelled of the spirit. These are the men through
whom the spirit works.

In other words, the Comforter convicts men of sin through the
activities of the church as it preaches the gospel.

The Lord says to go into all the world with the gospel, because it is as believers preach the gospel to men that the spirit convicts unbelievers.

Therefore, when Paul said the unbeliever would worship God, he meant that the saints in the assembly would preach the accurate knowledge of God, which the unbeliever would receive rather than resists.

> **The indwelling of the spirit is the reality of the worship of God.**

The expression "falling down on his face he will worship God" is another way of saying that the unbeliever abandons unbelief towards the gospel and reports that God is truly in the believer. At this point the unbeliever has turned from unbelief towards faith in God.

By the preaching of the word, the former unbeliever believes to receive the spirit as total cleansing and membership in the new nation.

Thus, Paul's "and so falling down on his face he will worship God" (see 1 Corinthians 14:25), is his way of instructing the church to co-labour with God to bring the unbeliever to the knowledge of God rather than operating tongues in a way that hardens the unbeliever. This ministry of the saints is how God offers the unbeliever a way out of unbelief.

Paul's quotation of Isaiah shows that the one speaking in another (**heteros**) tongues speaks for God and is a sign to the ones who have not received God's rest in Zion. In their unbelief, they conclude that the speaker in tongues is mad! Paul doesn't want the speaker in tongues to leave things this way or to operate in such a way that the unbeliever concludes with "you are mad". The unbeliever's conclusion shows the hardened heart of unbelief which cannot praise God in tongues as a language of devotion but instead concludes with "you are mad".

Paul charges the speaker in tongues to add interpretation to their tongues so that the unbeliever now sees the activity of God in the new covenant witnessed in the new tongues.

Through interpreted tongues, the unbelievers are rescued from their unbelief by giving them the chance to hear a clear message.

In 1 Corinthians 14:2,14-17, Paul had taught the Corinthians that tongues is a means of speaking to God in devotion. The speaker is not attacking anyone in a literal sense as a foreign army would have done in Isaiah's day.

However, from the perspective of the unbeliever who is present where tongues are spoken, the unbeliever who is observing the saints speak in tongues is observing a sign, for he cannot speak to God in tongues for devotion. He doesn't understand and cannot participate in such devotion on account of his unbelief.

What is the judgment in Isaiah 28?

15. Because ye have said, We have made a covenant with death, and with hell are we at agreement; when the overflowing scourge shall pass through, it shall not come unto us: for we have made lies our refuge, and under falsehood have we hid ourselves: 16. Therefore thus saith the Lord GOD, Behold, I lay in Zion for a foundation a **STONE**, a tried stone, a precious corner stone, a sure foundation: he that believeth shall not make haste. 17. Judgment also will I lay to the line, and righteousness to the plummet: and the hail shall sweep away the refuge of lies, and the waters shall overflow the hiding place.
Isaiah 28:15-17

This Judgment is God's work. Hail shall sweep away the refuge of lies. The waters shall overflow the hiding place (verse 15), which is the protection that men find in falsehood. This promised destruction of the refuge of lies and the hiding place of falsehood is not evil. It is good. It is God's judgment.

What is this judgment? God's judgment is the "sure foundation" that He lays in Zion so that a man might believe.

Isaiah used prophetic language rich in imagery to describe what happens when a man goes from unbelief to belief in the work God does in laying a foundation in Zion. Belief in God's word destroys the refuge of lies and the hiding place of falsehood. The man who did not originally believe is now a believing one.

In this light, the tongues being spoken is a judgment to unbelievers, who see the believer speaking in tongues as foreigners who shut the unbelievers in their unbelief. The unbeliever is hardened in unbelief for he does not understand what is being said.

Isaiah's prophecy sheds light on Acts 2:

4. And they were all filled with the Holy Ghost, and began to speak with other tongues, as the Spirit gave them utterance.
Acts 2:4

Those who had been taught by Jesus (in Acts1:5) began to speak in "other" tongues.

11. Cretes and Arabians, we do hear them speak in our tongues the wonderful works of God.
Acts 2:11

The crowd heard the disciples speak of the wonderful works of God.

The Jews that gathered when the 120 spoke in tongues were

men that had come to Jerusalem for the feast of Pentecost. They should have understood that Christ is the Passover from 50 days before. In unbelief, they failed to recognise that the ancient promise had been fulfilled.

> 12. And they were all amazed, and were in doubt, saying one to another, What meaneth this?
> Acts 2:12

These men were in doubt and amazement because they were in unbelief.

Although these men were identified as Galileans (see Acts 2:7), their "another" tongue distinguished them as being from another nation. Thus, Isaiah 28:11's men of "another tongue" were men of another nation but who were not from a distant land, physically speaking.

Salvation in Zion is the other nation, and speaking in tongues is the sign to the gathered Jews that believing the gospel is how God distinguishes men.

Since the crowd was amazed, while those who spoke in tongues were not said to be amazed, the amazed crowd, who were not speaking in tongues, were being made aware that they were not of that holy nation.

The solution?

> 14. But Peter, standing up with the eleven, lifted up his voice, and said unto them, Ye men of Judaea, and all **YE** that dwell at Jerusalem, be this known unto you, and hearken to my words:
> Acts 2:14

Peter got up and preached the gospel.

> 21. And it shall come to pass, **THAT** whosoever shall call on

> the name of the Lord shall be saved.
>
> Acts 2:21

Peter, who had just spoken in tongues, now instructed the crowd to call upon the name of the Lord for salvation (see Acts 2:21). He explained that God had raised Jesus from the dead (see Acts 2:32), and by raising Christ from the dead, God had made Jesus both Lord and Christ (see Acts 2:36). Now remission of sins was offered to them in the name (or accomplishment) of Jesus (see Acts 2:38). If they repented (or changed their minds from unbelief), they would receive the gift of the Holy Ghost as salvation (see Acts 2:38).

Therefore, those that believed the gospel would come out of the judgment of unbelief by receiving the gift of the Holy Ghost in salvation, and in that gift, they would speak in "another" tongue.

As speakers in tongues, they become the sign to the others in their midst that did not believe.

4

COVET EARNESTLY

By carefully observing the opening and closing statements of 1 Corinthians 12, we notice an interesting fact.

1. Now concerning spiritual **GIFTS**, brethren, I would not have you ignorant. 2. Ye know that ye were Gentiles, carried away unto these dumb idols, even as ye were led.
1 Corinthians 12:1-2

In opening verses of 1 Corinthians 12, when Paul wrote "I would not have you ignorant", he was saying that the saints were not giving their minds to understand spirituals as taught in the gospel and, as a result, they were not properly exercising the distinct vocal ability or new tongues that they had in the indwelling spirit.

The word translated "ignorant" is a word that means being unpersuadable towards that right knowledge of spirituals that they had been taught by the apostles.

Paul's closing remarks in 1 Corinthians 12 were:
31. But covet earnestly the best gifts: and yet shew I unto you a more excellent way.
1 Corinthians 12:31

Firstly, Paul had talked about gifts in verse 4 where he had taught that "Now there are diversities of gifts, but the same Spirit" (1

Corinthians 12:4).

It is these same gifts he taught the saints to "covet earnestly" in his closing remarks.

> 4. Now there are diversities of gifts, but the same Spirit.
> 1 Corinthians 12:4

First, we believed the gospel, which itself is called spiritual (the Greek word is **pneumatikos**) – see 1 Corinthians 9:11.

Then, in believing, we received the spirit (the Greek word is pneuma). From the gospel (**pneumatikos**).

The Greek word translated gift is **charisma**, a supernatural faculty. It is a stewardship, an endowment. Either you have it or never had it. Once had you this faculty, you can never stop having it. This ability is permanent. Basically, **Charisma** means that the ability is with you, and "that which you have received is yours". Therefore, it speaks of abilities that reside in the recipient once received.

Charisma refers to ability by the spirit's indwelling.

Since kinds of tongues are by the spirit, this means that the man speaking in tongues is expressing the spirit's indwelling.

We could also say that **charisma** refers to that which you are to use knowing you are a steward. You are responsible for its use.

There is a variety or diversities to the **charisma** (gifts) in the indwelling spirit. Thus, the moment we received the gospel, we became stewards of the **charisma** we possessed in eternal life.

Observe that it is the same Greek word, **charisma**, that has been translated as "gifts" in both verses 4 and 31. Also recall that **charisma** means you are to treat the abilities as your possession with no strings attached.

Given the command to "covet earnestly the best gifts" in 1 Corinthians 12:31, Paul's "I would not have you ignorant" in 1 Corinthians 12:1 is not a wish but a communication of knowledge
binding on the saints.

Let's observe Paul's conclusion again:
31. But covet earnestly the best gifts: and yet shew I unto you a
        more excellent way.
                    1 Corinthians 12:31

Paul did not end his teaching in chapter 12 as we would have
expected him to. If he was emphasizing the truth concerning
Christ and the church, he could have said, "covet earnestly the
best offices, people, etc" or something similar. However, he
ended with "covet the best gifts" and not "covet the best saints
or people".

Since Paul concluded with "covet earnestly the best gifts", it
would mean that up till that point he had been discussing the
various gifts.

Given his closing charge to covet the best gifts, his notoriously
tricky closing questions in 1 Corinthians 12 are to be examined
from the standpoint that he was discussing the gifts that he had
affirmed much earlier as being in diversity. Thus, Paul had not
been discussing Christ and the church.

His use of terms demands our attention. Our understanding of
the terms used must match his conclusion - "covet earnestly the
best gifts".

He was teaching "covet earnestly the best gifts" in his famous
metaphor:

Understanding Paul's metaphor

14. For the body is not one member, but many. 15. If the foot
shall say, Because I am not the hand, I am not of the body; is it
therefore not of the body? 16. And if the ear shall say, Because
I am not the eye, I am not of the body; is it therefore not of
the body? 17. If the whole body **WERE** an eye, where **WERE**
the hearing? If the whole **WERE** hearing, where **WERE** the
smelling? 18. But now hath God set the members every one of
them in the body, as it hath pleased him. 19. And if they were
all one member, where **WERE** the body? 20. But now **ARE
THEY** many members, yet but one body. 21. And the eye
cannot say unto the hand, I have no need of thee: nor again
the head to the feet, I have no need of you.
1 Corinthians 12:14-21

What is Paul's context for this metaphor?

The expression "If the foot shall say" does not make biological
sense when taken literally. The foot does not speak. However,
the foot that Paul referred to speaks. Therefore, this is a parable.

Paul repeatedly spoke of "the body" (in verses 14 to 20) and of
"the spirit" or "the same spirit" (in verses 4,7,8,9,11).

The singular body corresponds to "the one or selfsame spirit".

The abilities to say, hear, and smell are ways of representing the
many members which are the diversities in the gifts of the spirit.

The expression "the eye cannot say unto the hand, I have no
need of thee: nor again the head to the feet, I have no need of
you" means that the saint is to avail himself or herself of "all
these" that the spirit worketh (see 1 Corinthians 12:11).

11. But all these worketh that one and the selfsame Spirit,
dividing to every man severally as he will.
1 Corinthians 12:11

The same spirit (which is the one body in the parable of verse
20) works "all these" gifts of the spirit, which are in diversities.
Since the spirit is in men, it is men that put these abilities into
operation. Where a man is not present, these abilities are not
exerted or seen in operation. This means that these abilities are
worked by and through men.

For instance, the same spirit that is the ability of diversities of
tongues is also the ability of interpretation of tongues. Since the
spirit that gives the ability of tongues and its interpretation is in
men, the man that speaks in tongues also can interpret tongues.

Thus, whenever we hear a message in tongues, we can be sure
that the tongues did not voice itself independent of a human
speaker. A man voiced it.

Similarly, when we hear the interpretation of a message that has
been previously given in tongues, the interpretation does not
roll into the hearing of the assembly independent of a human
speaker. A man has to voice it.

Without proper instruction and willingness, it would seem addressing the saints publicly in tongues and giving the interpretation has passed away. When such happens, the truth is that the
saints are either ignorant about abilities possessed in the spirit
or they are unyielding to the indwelling spirit.

What was the point Paul was making just before he said "For
the body is not one member, but many" in 1 Corinthians 12:14?

11. But all these worketh that one and the selfsame Spirit,
dividing to every man severally as he will.
1 Corinthians 12:11

The point he had been making, which led to the parable was "all these worketh that one and the selfsame Spirit".

What are the "all these" that the spirit "worketh"?

They refer to the list in verses 8-10. Paul had said that the gifts were in differences, varieties, or diversities.

When he says, "now are they many members, yet but one body", we remember he had said "there are diversities of gifts, but the same Spirit" (see 1 Corinthians 12:4). Thus, the diversities of gifts correspond to "many members" in the parable.

In the same parable, "but one body" corresponds to "the same spirit".

> 17. If the whole body **WERE** an eye, where **WERE** the hearing? If the whole **WERE** hearing, where **WERE** the smelling?
> 1 Corinthians 12:17

The term "the whole body" represents the one spirit, while the eye, hearing, and smelling are the varieties, diversities of differences. The point is that the spirit is not to be limited to one diversity. The gifts are in the spirit and as stewards, we take all that is available and we use it responsibly for God's glory.

Thus, the context, overall argument, and conclusion of 1 Corinthians 12 demand that the members of the body are the gifts that we are to blend in expression.

Therefore, Paul used the parable about members of a body to show that though the gifts have their differences, they should be used together, because that is the way to achieve the purpose of the Lord for making us stewards of the gifts in the spirit.

The truth of the members of the body of Christ and Christ

makes the casual reader to read that truth into this chapter. However, Paul was not discussing Christ and the saints but the varieties in the gifts, which are to be exercised together.

What are the many members in the one body

20. But now **ARE THEY** many members, yet but one body.
1 Corinthians 12:20

This is describing the diverse gifts in the one spirit received at salvation by all saints.

Although there is one spirit, there is more than one gift. Paul's point is to let these diversities in the spirit operate together.

30. Have all the gifts of healing? do all speak with tongues? do all interpret?
1 Corinthians 12:30

Paul was continuing the point he had started in verse 11 about the spirit working all these gifts. Already, he had made the point that "If the whole body were an eye, where were the hearing? If the whole were hearing, where were the smelling?" (see 1 Corinthians 12:17).

The implied answer to these questions is "No".

So, Paul had made a case that the indwelling spirit in each saint is the various abilities listed in verses 8-10. However, not all speak in tongues, exercise the gifts of healings, or interpret tongues as they should when the saints are gathered.

Even though there are varieties in the one spirit and that each saint is to be a good steward of all the abilities in the spirit, the Corinthians were ignorant of these facts or were ignoring the knowledge that Paul taught. They were still operating by their pagan beliefs when they were led unto dumb idols. So Paul made the point that not all operated as good stewards of the spirit's riches.

Furthermore, when Paul said "but covet earnestly the best gifts: and yet shew I unto you a more excellent way" (1 Corinthians 12:31, he was continuing the singular thread of thought he had been communicating. He was not discussing the saints and membership in the body of Christ but the exercising of the gifts together to maximize the benefit to the saints.

5

WHAT CHARITY DOES

7. So that ye come behind in no gift; waiting for the coming of
our Lord Jesus Christ:
1 Corinthians 1:7

By Paul's admission, the Corinthians did not come behind in any gift. The Greek word for gift is **charisma**, which speaks of abilities by the spirit's indwelling.

6. Now, brethren, if I come unto you speaking with tongues,
what shall I profit you, except I shall speak to you either by
revelation, or by knowledge, or by prophesying, or by doctrine?
1 Corinthians 14:6

We know they did not come behind in any gift because, according to Paul the Corinthians were already coming to one another speaking with tongues.

He did not need to encourage the Corinthians to speak in tongues. They were already given to that.

What then was the challenge?

1. Now concerning spiritual **GIFTS**, brethren, I would not
have you ignorant.
1 Corinthians 12:1

> **"**
> *As saints, we follow*
> *after charity with*
> *our minds and*
> *the word on our*
> *minds is what later*
> *transforms into our*
> *practice.*
> **"**

Observe that although the Corinthians did not come behind in any gift, and Paul had identified that the Corinthians were speaking in tongues, he affirmed that they were ignorant. This meant that they were unpersuadable towards that right knowledge of spirituals that they had been taught by the apostles through the gospel.

Thus, Paul distinguished between speaking in tongues and possessing the vital knowledge needed for unleashing its power. For us Paul's stance shows that even in the matter of spirituals, the believer is a disciple of the written word and improves his administration of utterance by increasing his word in-take.

Paul did not tell them to just do whatever they fancied. What was his response to their ignorance?

Paul said, "I give you to understand" (see 1 Corinthians 12:3).

What were they ignorant about?

> 6. Now, brethren, if I come unto you speaking with tongues, what shall I profit you, except I shall speak to you either by revelation, or by knowledge, or by prophesying, or by doctrine?
> 1 Corinthians 14:6

They were ignorant concerning the proper exercise of speaking in tongues to bring profit.

Love is God's action

Reading through 1 Corinthians 13 and 14, charity is a recurring term

1. Though I speak with the tongues of men and of angels, and have not charity, I am become as sounding brass, or a tinkling cymbal. 2. And though I have **THE GIFT** of prophecy, and understand all mysteries, and all knowledge; and though I have all faith, so that I could remove mountains, and have not charity, I am nothing. 3. And though I bestow all my goods to feed **THE POOR**, and though I give my body to be burned, and have not charity, it profiteth me nothing.

1 Corinthians 13:1-3

In each of the first three verses of 1 Corinthians 13, Paul repeated the term "have not charity", for emphasis. "Have not charity" was Paul's statement of the problem among the Corinthians. He also had this to say about charity in the next chapter:

1. Follow after charity, and desire spiritual **GIFTS**, but rather that ye may prophesy.

1 Corinthians 14:1

Again, we see the word "charity". This time, it is not "have not charity" but to "follow after charity".

The Greek word translated charity in the KJV is the word **agape**, which is usually translated as "love". Thus, Paul's "have not charity" can be rendered "have not love" and "follow after charity" can be rendered "follow after love". Follow after charity means to make love your aim.

> *One can succeed at making sounds associated with tongues, while failing to bless the audience.*

1 Corinthians 14 is teaching concerning our love walk towards other saints.

16. Hereby perceive we the love **OF** God, because he laid down his life for us: and we ought to lay down **OUR** lives for the brethren.

1 John 3:16

Our love walk towards other saints derives from God's love towards us in Christ laying down His life for us.

God's love refers to His action in redemption. Our love for the saints is the product of perceiving God's love in Christ.

20. I am crucified with Christ: nevertheless I live; yet not I, but Christ liveth in me: and the life which I now live in the flesh I live by the faith of the Son of God, who loved me, and gave himself for me.

Galatians 2:20

Again, we observe that God's love for man is seen as His action of giving Himself for men.

16. For God so loved the world, that he gave his only begotten Son, that whosoever believeth in him should not perish, but have everlasting life.

John 3:16

God's love is His giving of His only begotten Son in the resurrection as the life of the man that believes the gospel.

> **Our love walk towards other saints derives from God's love towards us in Christ laying down His life for us.**

The knowledge of this love works on our minds and makes us lay "down our lives for the brethren". Just as Jesus served us for our benefit, we neither serve others for our benefit nor boast about it. Rather we serve for the benefit of others.

14. And as Moses lifted up the serpent in the wilderness, even
so must the Son of man be lifted up: 15. That whosoever
believeth in him should not perish, but have eternal life.
John 3:14-15

How did God give His Son to us? The explanation is that God
gave His Son in the Son of Man being lifted up, His resurrection
from the dead.

9. That if thou shalt confess with thy mouth the Lord Jesus,
and shalt believe in thine heart that God hath raised him from
the dead, thou shalt be saved.
Romans 10:9

When we believed in our hearts that "God hath raised him from
the dead", we received that resurrection as God's love into our
hearts.

2. And walk in love, as Christ also hath loved us, and hath
given himself for us an offering and a sacrifice to God for a
sweet smelling savour.
Ephesians 5:2

So "Christ also hath loved us" and "hath given himself for us"
are not two different ideas but one. "Christ also hath loved us",
which is to say He "hath given himself for us".

Observe again that Christ's love for us is that He "hath given
himself for us".

As we give our minds to this fact of His love, it becomes a walk
of love through us to other saints. Now, we walk in love.

1. Be ye, therefore, followers of God, as dear children;
Ephesians 5:1

The word translated "followers" in "be ye, therefore, followers of God" means "to imitate" or "to mimic".

We follow, mimic, or imitate God "as dear children". It is because we are His dear children that we can imitate Him in love.

Follow after charity

1. Follow after charity, and desire spiritual **GIFTS**, but rather that ye may prophesy.
1 Corinthians 14:1

> **Utterance is the pursuit of God's love in sounds. In it we demonstrate towards our brethren that same service found in Christ.**

Therefore, when Paul said "Follow after charity", it was because we are "followers of God, as dear children". In following the love of God, we prophesy.

We have shown that our prophecy provides a way out for the unbeliever out of his unbelief.

Thus, in 1 Corinthians 13:1-3, "have not love" means not following God by not co-labouring with Him. It means not allowing God's actions in Christ to inform our actions towards all men, especially the saints.

Given his command to "follow after charity" in 1 Corinthians 14:1, everything else Paul said in the rest of 1 Corinthians 14 was an extensive teaching on what following after charity looks like in practice.

Here is another thing Paul said about charity in 1 Corinthians 13:

4. Charity suffereth long, **AND** is kind; charity envieth not; charity vaunteth not itself, is not puffed up,

1 Corinthians 13:4

Charity is not puffed up. This shows that "puff up" is the opposite of charity. Whatever charity is, "puff up" is not.

Observe that before his teaching in 1 Corinthians 12, 13, and 14, Paul had taught the Corinthians earlier using this term "charity":

1. Now as touching things offered unto idols, we know that we all have knowledge. Knowledge puffeth up, but charity edifieth.
1 Corinthians 8:1

Although, Paul said "Knowledge puffeth up, but charity edifieth", he was not contrasting knowledge and love. How are we sure? He had already said, "we know that we all have knowledge".

That expression "we all have knowledge" means that all the people that Paul addressed in verse 1 had knowledge. Thus, knowledge was the commonality.

What Paul wanted to demonstrate was knowledge without love contrasted with knowledge devoid of love. Knowledge with love is knowledge used for the edification of others. Since the love of God is God giving Himself to us in redemption, Paul taught about giving ourselves for the benefit of others.

10 For if any man see thee which hast knowledge sit at meat in the idol's temple, shall not the conscience of him which is weak be emboldened to eat those things which are offered to idols;
11 And through thy knowledge shall the weak brother perish, for whom Christ died? 12 But when ye sin so against the brethren, and wound their weak conscience, ye sin against Christ.
1 Corinthians 8:10-12

There is no doubt that this man (representing the Corinthians) has knowledge – the knowledge had been stated in 1 Corinthians 8:4-6.

Paul's warning was stated as "through thy knowledge shall the weak brother perish". The knowledge was not the issue but the use of the knowledge. Rather than use the knowledge to edify the brethren by preferring them in love, this brother was selfish, not caring about the conscience of others.

Paul had the same knowledge. However, he did not use it selfishly.

> 13 Wherefore, if meat make my brother to offend, I will eat no flesh while the world standeth, lest I make my brother to offend.
> 1 Corinthians 8:13

Paul used the same knowledge to edify the brethren whose conscience another knowledgeable brother had ignored. His choice, in God's love, was "if meat make my brother to offend, I will eat no flesh while the world standeth". He made this choice so that he would not wound the conscience of the brethren. He has preferred them in love. This is knowledge edifying.

The opposite scenario is knowledge puffing up (1 Corinthians 8:10-12).

Since "puff up" is the opposite of charity, and charity edifies others, it means that puffing up is the absence of edification of others (those in our audience).

Paul wanted to show that knowledge could be possessed in two ways – as knowledge alone, which puffed up, and knowledge submitted to charity that edified another.

Here is another thing Paul said about charity to the Galatians:

13. For, brethren, ye have been called unto liberty; only USE not liberty for an occasion to the flesh, but by love serve one another.

Galatians 5:13

That word translated love is the same word translated charity in other verses. So, love (or charity) serves another.

We know from the 1 Corinthians 13:4 text that the opposite of charity is "puff up". To "have love" means to serve or to give service. To "have not charity" means not to serve others. It means to be "puffed up". Since charity edifies and charity is service, charity is our service of ministering edification to others.

> **The ability to speak in tongues is not a phonetic ability taught in language schools by men. It is spoken by the power of Christ resident in His saints.**

Thus, based on 1 Corinthians 8:1, knowledge can be used to edify others or not edify others. When knowledge is not used to serve or edify others, that is "knowledge puffs up". When knowledge is used to serve others, that is charity or love.

We navigate 1 Corinthians 12, 13, and 14 with this understanding of charity from 1 Corinthians 8, 1 Corinthians 13, and Galatians 5.

Recall that Paul's stated problem among the Corinthians was:

1. Though I speak with the tongues of men and of angels, and have not charity, I am become as sounding brass, or a tinkling cymbal.

1 Corinthians 13:1

We know that "have not love" or "have not charity" is not having the edification of our audience in mind.

Examining "have not love"

3. And though I bestow all my goods to feed **THE POOR**,
and though I give my body to be burned, and have not charity,
it profiteth me nothing.
1 Corinthians 13:3

Let us look more closely at the setting in which the term "have
not charity" is used.

Charity means to serve another with the advantage or edification of that person in mind. So, "have not charity" while "I
bestow all my goods" and "I give my body to be burned" means
that all my deeds are without the aim of edification of others
in mind.

Both "my goods" and "my body" are visible things; "bestow all
my goods" and giving "my body to be burned" all look like acts
of love but Paul asked the reader to look a little closer.

This is the New English Translation of the same text:
If I give away everything I own, and if I give over my body in
order to boast, but do not have love, I receive no benefit.
1 Corinthians 13:3 (NET)

People can see "everything I own" and "my body" but the expression "in order to boast" shows that what I gave was the
intent in my heart. It looked like I was giving the way God gives
in love and not for self but in reality, I was boasting.

Where the KJV says "it profiteth me nothing", the NET says "I
receive no benefit"

Given that charity means to serve another with the advantage or
edification of that other person in mind, charity is not for your
benefit. Thus, "it profiteth me nothing", or "I receive no benefit" is concerning our service to others. Our benefit or profit

would be those lives helped along and edified by our ministry.

When motives are contrary to Christ, we forfeit this benefit, since we would be manipulating men under the guise of blessing them. Such a person is putting on a show "in order to boast". When things are done to boast, the person with the impure motive is unable to receive the benefit of serving others.

In utterance, our Christ-given gain is to serve men.

Here is the same verse in another translation:
> Even if I dole out all that I have [to the poor in providing] food, and if I surrender my body to be burned or in order that I may glory, but have not love (God's love in me), I gain nothing.
> 1 Corinthians 13:3 (AMPC)

This version brings out the idea that "if I surrender my body to be burned" means "in order that I may glory". This speaks of motive.

Here is another translation:
> If I give all I possess to the poor and give over my body to hardship that I may boast, but do not have love, I gain nothing
> 1 Corinthians 13:3 (NIV)

Instead of King James', "if I surrender my body to be burned", The manuscripts used by the NIV states "that I may boast".

When we follow after charity or act in the light of Christ's service, we minister utterance as love's service to those believers who are our audience. In a setting of "have not charity", the motivation is "that I may boast".

A saint can go through the motion of speaking tongues to address the saints but his motive has killed the edification mandate. What is heard is tongues. What is done in the heart is boasting.

It is about the speaker's prowess and not about maximising the benefit to the audience.

What is the answer to this "have not love"?

It is right in the next chapter.

> 1. Follow after charity, and desire spiritual **GIFTS**, but rather that ye may prophesy.
> 1 Corinthians 14:1

What is meant by "follow after charity"?

Charity or love of God is the sacrifice of Christ which the believer has already received as the indwelling spirit by the gospel. The saint is not following after charity to believe. For the man that has believed, following after charity is a thing of knowledge. As saints, we follow after charity with our minds and the word on our minds is what later transforms into our practice.

When we have believed the truth of the sacrifice of Christ, we are to continually give our minds to this truth, so that it becomes our slant in ministry to others. This is charity, the knowledge of God's love informing yours. The saints that do not give their minds to these facts, would find that they are not ministering from that slant to the brethren.

Given that charity has to do with pursuing the edification of others, the term "follow after charity" means being guided by the edification of others. It is another way of saying, "follow after the edification of others" or "make the edification of others your aim". It is to follow the example of Christ's love.

We are to think of utterance as serving others so that edification might come forth.

Since prophesying is the practice of following after charity, prophesying is taught as our practice in the knowledge of the service of Christ who laid down His life for us. This prophesying is based on the knowledge of the service of Christ who laid down His life for us.

Paul taught prophesying as the core of his great teaching on love which started in 1 Corinthians 13. In fact, his treatment of prophecy as the practice of redemptive love meant that redemption and prophesying go together. We put the knowledge gleaned in our studies in redemption to use in utterance.

You could put it this way, that when you prophesy, you have walked in love.

If prophecy is the love walk, what does that say about the saint that refuses to prophesy? Such a saint has not attempted to practice the love of God in utterance.

Utterance is the pursuit of God's love in sounds. In it we demonstrate towards our brethren that same service found in Christ.

In the gospel, we see that God became a man amongst men to save men. This is our teaching on God's love. The lesson that we learn in the service of God in Christ is that God uses men to edify men. Salvation implies utterance, for the same spirit in the Saviour by which He saved the people is at work in the saints for the edification of other saints.

With this in mind, we give ourselves fully to the service of utterance so that the edification that God has in mind for the saints is realized. Utterance then becomes the pursuit or practice of love by the man that has been loved by God in the gospel. This means that salvation and utterance go hand in hand.

Utterance is to be our service in the knowledge of the service of Christ who laid down His life for us. Therefore, Paul presented utterance as the practice of love, teaching utterance as "follow after charity".

With charity (or love) linked with prophecy, Paul's use of charity in 1 Corinthians 13 and 14 was with utterance in mind.

Furthermore, in 1 Corinthians 14, Paul answered the question "what will the love of Christ look like on the matter of utterance?" or "how do you follow charity on the matter of utterance?"

Paul was teaching the love walk in 1 Corinthians 12, 13, and 14.

It is the love walk seen in the way we administer our words when we flow in the spirit of God. Paul wanted us to know what the love of God does when we address the assembly.

1. Though I speak with the tongues of men and of angels, and have not charity, I am become **AS** sounding brass, or a tinkling cymbal.
1 Corinthians 13:1

This "speak" in "though I speak with the tongues of men and of angels, and have not charity" is lacking in the love of God. It is not obeying the 1 Corinthians 14:1 command to "follow after charity".

It is possible to speak in tongues and "have not love" (have not the edification of saints and clarification to the unbeliever in mind). However, this should not be the case but it happens.

1. Follow after charity, and desire spiritual **GIFTS**, but rather that ye may prophesy.
1 Corinthians 14:1

This term "follow after charity", shows that the term "have not love" used earlier in 1 Corinthians 13:1 is not a reference to the believer being devoid of God's love. Instead, it speaks of the believer's pursuit – what is the believer using the knowledge of the gospel for. "Have not love" means that the saint who has received God's love is not allowing that love to guide one's interaction with other saints to edify them.

Although while ministering to the audience we speak in tongues, we only do so because speaking in tongues is a means of bringing edification to the saints. We follow after charity and not after the sound of tongues.

The man who makes tongues his aim will conclude that the job is done once tongues is spoken to the assembly. Whereas the man who has made love the aim knows that the tongues spoken to the assembly is a means to an end and that the job is undone for as long as the saints are not edified. Such a person is sounding brass or useless noise. The clanging cymbal is a musical instrument that is not giving pleasant music.

As saints, we are not following tongues. We are focusing on charity (the love of God in action). This means that our action of speaking in tongues was not just to speak in tongues to the audience – that would be showing off. We are loving the saints using tongues to convey the love. Love gives. In this case, love is the giving of the meaning of the sounds (tongues).

"I am become as sounding brass, or a tinkling cymbal" means I don't do love's job of giving edification to the audience who have heard the sound of tongues. The speaker in tongues knows that the audience hearing of tongues is not edification. "Having love" only comes after speaking to (or addressing) the people in tongues. It is serving edification to those who have heard the tongues.

1. Though I speak with the tongues of men and of angels, and have not charity, I am become **AS** sounding brass, or a tinkling cymbal.
1 Corinthians 13:1

"Have not love" means rather than minister to them, I came to the people with a show, for my administration of utterance is lacking in actions that bless the audience who have heard the speaker address them in tongues.

When Paul spoke of "sounding brass, or a tinkling cymbal" was he instructing the Corinthians about the theatre or taking them in an advanced class on music? Of course, he was not. Paul had not suddenly become a conductor of music at the opera or orchestra. His subject matter had not changed. He had said in 1 Corinthians 12:1 "Now concerning spiritual gifts, brethren, I would not have you ignorant". He was writing about spirituals.

The terms "sounding brass and tinkling cymbal" meant that Paul had used musical instruments as a figure of speech. In this illustration, there were instruments which are seen but not giving any meaningful music. The sounds that came forth were unpleasant. This was the same thing as producing sounds just for the sake of sounds, thereby defeating the purpose of the instruments.

Paul was therefore tackling the issue of the sound of tongues being heard without the speaker giving service to the saints.

By using the love of God to explain addressing people in tongues, Paul showed that the speaker in tongues could give voluminous utterances, without getting the job done. In other words, one can succeed at making sounds associated with tongues, while failing to bless the audience.

It is these same gifts he taught the saints to "covet earnestly" in his closing remarks.

6

GIVEN BY THE SPIRIT

8. For to one is given by the Spirit the word of wisdom; to
another the word of knowledge by the same Spirit; 9. To
another faith by the same Spirit; to another the gifts of healing
by the same Spirit; 10. To another the working of miracles; to
another prophecy; to another discerning of spirits; to another
DIVERS kinds of tongues; to another the interpretation of
tongues: 11. But all these worketh that one and the selfsame
Spirit, dividing to every man severally as he will.
1 Corinthians 12:8-11

As we have noted earlier, Paul taught the saints that the
word of wisdom, the word of knowledge, faith, the
gifts of healing, the working of miracles, prophecy,
divers kinds of tongues, and the interpretation of tongues are
given by the same Spirit.

Pay close attention to the fact that kinds of tongues and the interpretation of tongues are given by the same indwelling-spirit.
Also observe that in the bible, all the men that spoke in tongues
are believers in the gospel, all were new creation men.

Further, we have previously noted that just as with the kinds of
tongues, the interpretation of tongues is given by the indwelling
spirit of God. Both the ability to speak in tongues and the ability to interpret what has been spoken in tongues are God-given
by the spirit of God indwelling the speaker.

> **Edification is targeted at the mind, therefore it is a thing of understanding, which usually comes by interpretation of tongues.**

The ability to speak in tongues is not a phonetic ability taught in language schools by men. It is spoken by the power of Christ resident in His saints.

According to Jesus, tongues are a sign of the gospel which has been believed by the speaker (see Mark 16:17-18).

The interpretation of tongues gives the meaning of things that have been said supernaturally in tongues.

What is required for a man to speak in tongues?

17. And these signs shall follow them that believe; In my name shall they cast out devils; they shall speak with new tongues;
Mark 16:17

14. Now when the apostles which were at Jerusalem heard that Samaria had received the word of God, they sent unto them Peter and John: 15. Who, when they were come down, prayed for them, that they might receive the Holy Ghost:
Acts 8:14-15

Both the instructions of Jesus and the practice of the church as recorded by Luke in Acts show that the only requirement is that the man or woman should have heard the gospel and believed it.

How long after salvation before a man can speak in tongues?

44. While Peter yet spake these words, the Holy Ghost fell
on all them which heard the word. 45. And they of the
circumcision which believed were astonished, as many as came
with Peter, because that on the Gentiles also was poured out
the gift of the Holy Ghost. 46. For they heard them speak with
tongues, and magnify God. Then answered Peter,

Acts 10:44-46

In Cornelius' house, while Peter was preaching, Cornelius and
his household were so ready for the gospel that before Peter
finished preaching they had believed and had started speaking
in tongues.

Isn't Cornelius' kind of speaking in tongues fake or counterfeit?

46. For they heard them speak with tongues, and magnify God.
Then answered Peter, 47. Can any man forbid water, that these
should not be baptized, which have received the Holy Ghost
as well as we?

Acts 10:46-47

15. And as I began to speak, the Holy Ghost fell on them, as
on us at the beginning. 16. Then remembered I the word of
the Lord, how that he said, John indeed baptized with water;
but ye shall be baptized with the Holy Ghost. 17. Forasmuch
then as God gave them the like gift as **HE DID** unto us, who
believed on the Lord Jesus Christ; what was I, that I could
withstand God? 18. When they heard these things, they held
their peace, and glorified God, saying, Then hath God also to
the Gentiles granted repentance unto life.

Acts 11:15-18

No, they were not counterfeit. Peter accepted Cornelius' utterance and even used it as proof to the other apostles that God had extended salvation to non-Jews.

Don't some Christians speak fake tongues?

None of the apostles wrote anything about fake tongues. If they existed, then the apostles would have written about it.

Who determines how long after salvation before we speak in tongues?

9. And he was three days without sight, and neither did eat nor drink.
Acts 9:9

11. And the Lord **SAID** unto him, Arise, and go into the street which is called Straight, and enquire in the house of Judas for **ONE** called Saul, of Tarsus: for, behold, he prayeth,
Acts 9:11

> *The responsibility of interpretation of the thanksgiving spoken to God in tongues sits with the speaker in tongues and not with the audience.*

17. And Ananias went his way, and entered into the house; and putting his hands on him said, Brother Saul, the Lord, **EVEN** Jesus, that appeared unto thee in the way as thou camest, hath sent me, that thou mightest receive thy sight, and be filled with the Holy Ghost.
Acts 9:17

Acts 9 shows that Ananias laid hands on Paul "be filled with the Holy Ghost".

18. I thank my God, I speak with tongues more than ye all:
1 Corinthians 14:18

Paul spoke in tongues after Ananias had laid hands on him, for he said, "I thank my God, I speak with tongues more than ye all".

Acts 9 shows that Paul spoke in tongues after he had prayed for three days and Ananias had laid hands on him.

> *The principle of edification commands that uninterpreted tongues is inappropriate when it is addressed to the church.*

In Acts 2 it took about 7 days after Jesus had taught the disciples before they started speaking in tongues. (Pentecost is 50 days after Passover. 3 days after Passover, Jesus rose, then He taught for 40 days. That leaves about 7 days or less).

14. Now when the apostles which were at Jerusalem heard that Samaria had received the word of God, they sent unto them Peter and John: 15. Who, when they were come down, prayed for them, that they might receive the Holy Ghost:
Acts 8:14-15

It was some time after the Samaritans had believed the gospel before Peter and John laid hands on them and they started speaking in tongues

4. Then said Paul, John verily baptized with the baptism of repentance, saying unto the people, that they should believe on him which should come after him, that is, on Christ Jesus. 5. When they heard **THIS**, they were baptized in the name of the Lord Jesus. 6. And when Paul had laid **HIS** hands upon them, the Holy Ghost came on them; and they spake with tongues, and prophesied. 7. And all the men were about

twelve.
Acts 19:4-7

Paul laid hands on the 12 men at Ephesus almost as soon as they believed the gospel and they started speaking in tongues.

15. And as I began to speak, the Holy Ghost fell on them, as
on us at the beginning.
Acts 11:15

44. While Peter yet spake these words, the Holy Ghost fell
on all them which heard the word. 45. And they of the
circumcision which believed were astonished, as many as came
with Peter, because that on the Gentiles also was poured out
the gift of the Holy Ghost. 46. For they heard them speak with
tongues, and magnify God. Then answered Peter,
Acts 10:44-46

Cornelius and his household started speaking in tongues immediately they heard the gospel.

Thus, there is no set time. The variation in the length of time is due to many factors dependent on man. The commonality is believing the gospel.

When do people begin to speak in tongues?

17. Then laid they **THEIR** hands on them, and they received
the Holy Ghost.
Acts 8:17

Men start talking in tongues the moment they "receive". This word "receive" means "to seize", "to take" or "lay hold of".

For a variety of reasons, men are ready to receive at different times. The common thread is that at whatever time men are ready to receive, they start speaking in tongues. All the pre-requisites that men tend to put in their path before they speak in tongues only give an indication of what triggers their receiving.

Must hands be laid for men to speak in tongues?

On the day of Pentecost and in Cornelius' house, no one laid hands on anyone to speak in tongues.

> 17. And Ananias went his way, and entered into the house; and putting his hands on him said, Brother Saul, the Lord, **EVEN** Jesus, that appeared unto thee in the way as thou camest, hath sent me, that thou mightest receive thy sight, and be filled with the Holy Ghost.
> Acts 9:17

Ananias laid hands on Paul, who he referred to as "brother Saul", so Paul might speak in tongues.

> 17. Then laid they **THEIR** hands on them, and they received the Holy Ghost. 18. And when Simon saw that through laying on of the apostles' hands the Holy Ghost was given, he offered them money,
> Acts 8:17-18

Peter and John laid hands on the saints at Samaria, who had believed the gospel, so they might speak in tongues.

> 6. And when Paul had laid **HIS** hands upon them, the Holy Ghost came on them; and they spake with tongues, and prophesied. 7. And all the men were about twelve.
> Acts 19:6-7

Paul laid hands on 12 men at Ephesus who had believed the gospel, then they spoke in tongues.

So, hands do not need to be laid. Belief in the gospel is the prerequisite.

Do we not have to breathe on people so they can speak in tongues?

John records (John 20:22) that "Jesus breathed on them, and saith unto them, Receive ye the Holy Ghost". Comparing John's record with that of Luke 24, Mark 16, Matthew 28, and Acts 1, this expression "breathed on them" corresponds to Jesus' teaching after the resurrection. Thus, it is a figurative way of saying He preached the gospel to them.

We must be sure that they have believed the gospel.

When is God going to speak in tongues for me?

4. And they were all filled with the Holy Ghost, and began to speak with other tongues, as the Spirit gave them utterance.
Acts 2:4

At Pentecost, it was men that spoke in tongues.

46. For they heard them speak with tongues, and magnify God. Then answered Peter,
Acts 10:46

In Cornelius' house, it was men that spoke in tongues.

6. And when Paul had laid **HIS** hands upon them, the Holy Ghost came on them; and they spake with tongues, and

prophesied.
Acts 19:6

Again, at Ephesus, it was men that spoke in tongues.

God is not the one speaking in tongues for us. It is men who have believed the gospel that do the speaking as they become conscious of God.

Should I wait to be excited before I speak in tongues?

Speaking in tongues has nothing to do with excitement or feelings. It is a sign of the gospel. We speak as often as we want to because we are stewards of the vocal ability of tongues.

When will God teach me how to make my tongues confuse the devil?

God is not out to make you confuse the devil. He wants you to stay away from confusion.

2. For he that speaketh in an **UNKNOWN** tongue speaketh not unto men, but unto God: for no man understandeth **HIM**; howbeit in the spirit he speaketh mysteries.
1 Corinthians 14:2

Tongues is not designed to confuse the devil. It is primarily for communion with God.

Can a non-Christian speak in tongues?

There is no instance in all the epistles, the Gospels, or the book of Acts, where non-Christians spoke in tongues.

17. And these signs shall follow them that believe; In my name
shall they cast out devils; they shall speak with new tongues;
Mark 16:17

Jesus said that tongues would be spoken by those who believe.
Speaking in tongues is a sign that the speaker has believed the
gospel.

If a non-Christian mimics tongues is that not speaking in tongues?

It is only men that have believed the gospel that speak in tongues.

If the unsaved grab hold of the recording of a Christian speaking in tongues and the non-Christian correctly memorises the
sequence of sounds and can reproduce the sounds perfectly,
the non-Christian has still not spoken in tongues for tongues is
the vocal ability of the indwelling spirit received by the gospel.

Are other tongues spoken in the language of man?

Although prophecy and interpretation of tongues are spoken
in the known language of the audience, which would be the
languages of men, the weight of evidence from Paul's treatment
would indicate that tongues is not in human language.

The very fact that interpretation of tongues is an ability of the
spirit and not linguistic skills trained into the mind indicates that
tongues was not spoken in the languages of men.

What if the speaker in tongues makes sounds like to that found in human languages?

The proper name for tongues is "new tongues", indicating lingual abilities from the new birth or vocal abilities of the new creation man. It is also called "other tongues", indicating that it is a language other than by natural ability. Although we might hear men speak sounds that sound similar or exactly like the sounds or phonetics associated with human languages, tongues is totally of a divine origin.

> *Anyone can see a vision, but seeing accurately and saying accurately is not the same thing. Retelling accurately requires discipleship.*

The fact that it takes the supernatural ability of the spirit called interpretation of tongues to make sense of what has been spoken in tongues, it is also another clue that even if tongues sound similar to human language, it is not the language of men nor is it languages taught by men.

Did the crowd at Pentecost not understand the tongues spoken by the saints?

The answer is yes and no.

No, they did not understand the tongues itself for the understanding of tongues requires the demonstration of the spirit called interpretation of tongues before tongues can be understood.

In the bible, non-Christians do not exercise either tongues or interpretation of tongues.

Yes, we can say the crowd understood on the day of Pentecost but what they understood was not tongues. Peter explained what happened as prophecy. In that case, it was the interpretation of tongues that registered in the mind of the crowd.

What if a non-Christian hears what is said in tongues and interprets it to the audience?

> **Utterance has optimal impact when the hearers are disciples who prioritise the word. Such people can do a lot with little utterance.**

There is no instance in all the epistles, the synoptic Gospels (Matthew, Mark, Luke, or John), or even the book of Acts, where non-Christians were used to demonstrate the interpretation of tongues. Since in the scriptural records, the interpretation of tongues is always only spoken by saints, the idea of a non-Christian "interpreting" what has been said in tongues would be a sign. It would not be the interpretation of tongues.

A sign and wonder would have occurred in the hearing of such a non-Christian. On hearing the tongues, something has been quickened to him by the spirit of God.

Interestingly, in such a setting, the Christian that spoke the tongues can go ahead and interpret the tongues and what the Christian would say as the interpretation of tongues might very well be different from what the non-Christin experienced.

Two demonstrations of the spirit have coincided, but they are not the same thing.

In such a scenario, the Christian interpreted the tongues, while the non-Christin experienced a sign and wonder to arrest his or her attention. The trigger was hearing tongues.

That scenario where a non-Christian "interpreted" what has been said in tongues cannot be the interpretation of tongues. Scripturally speaking, the non-Christian did not understand the tongues at all.

7

THE EDIFICATION PRINCIPLE

11. For with stammering lips and another tongue will he
speak to this people. 12. To whom he said, This **IS** the rest
WHEREWITH ye may cause the weary to rest; and this **IS**
the refreshing: yet they would not hear.
Isaiah 28:11-12

In the Genesis through Malachi text, the Hebrew word translated "rest" in "this is the rest" was used about 64 times, whereas the Hebrew word translated refreshing was used only once in the whole of the Hebrew scriptures!

The Passion translation reads:
   For he has said to them, "This is your rest, so let the weary
   rest; this is your comfort"—but they would not listen.
   Isaiah 28:12 (TPT)

What the KJV translates as "refreshing", the Passion translators recorded as comfort.

Given that Isaiah 28:11-12 is Paul's foundation for 1 Corinthians 14, taking the meaning of comfort from Isaiah 28:12 would explain how Paul defined prophecy.

3. But he that prophesieth speaketh unto men **TO** edification,
and exhortation, and comfort.
1 Corinthians 14:3

Prophecy is explained as edification, exhortation, and comfort.

> **Speaking in tongues of angels is speaking in tongues not as a prayer or communion with God but as a messenger to the assembly.**

The Greek word **kai** translated as "and" in "edification, and exhortation, and comfort" can be an explaining word or a connecting word. In this case, it is all tied to the explanation of prophecy. Therefore, the terms edification, exhortation, and comfort refer to the same thing. When Paul says prophesying, he means edification, which is expressed as exhortation, and comfort. So edification, exhortation, and comfort are not three things but one.

The word translated "edification" means to build. Therefore, the lesson is that God who built men as His habitation in Zion also builds or edifies men through men today in the local church.

1. Follow after charity, and desire spiritual **GIFTS**, but rather
that ye may prophesy.
1 Corinthians 14:1

Following after charity is further explained as desiring spiritual gifts. Since the word "gift" is italicized, the text says desire spiritual or desire the things of, in, by, or through the spirit.

Also, the word translated "rather" means "most especially". Thus, the text can be rendered as:

"desire spiritual or desire the things of, in, by or through the spirit most especially that ye may prophesy".

Paul is emphatic on prophesying.

The heart of Paul's teaching in 1 Corinthians 12, 13, and 14 could be summarized as "Follow after charity", which most especially prophesies. He was teaching about the love walk and using prophesying to illustrate his point.

This love walk is seen as rather or most especially "that ye may prophesy".

"Ye" is an old English pronoun for "all of you". The expression "Ye may prophesy" means that it is not a select few that possess this ability. All the saints possess this "ye may prophesy" ability. All are to do something with that ability.

How does Paul explain "ye may prophesy"?

> 3. But he that prophesieth speaketh unto men **TO** edification,
> and exhortation, and comfort.
> 1 Corinthians 14:3

Paul's prophesying is speaking edification to men.

Which men does Paul have in mind?

> 5. I would that ye all spake with tongues, but rather that ye
> prophesied: for greater **IS** he that prophesieth than he that
> speaketh with tongues, except he interpret, that the church
> may receive edifying.
> 1 Corinthians 14:5

Again, we see the expression "rather that ye prophesied", the same idea in 1 Corinthians 14:1 expanded upon.

The one that prophesies speaks so "the church may receive edifying".

This identifies the men receiving edification in verse 3 as the church in verse 5.

Thus, from both 1 Corinthians 14:3 and 1 Corinthians 14:5, we can safely say that when Paul uses prophecy, he has edification of the church in mind. So, we can replace prophesy with edification.

In the light of 1 Corinthians 14:3 and 14:5, the 1 Corinthians 14:1 condensed teaching can be restated as "rather that ye may speak edification to the church". To desire spirituals is to make a habit of speaking edification to the saints.

This means that Paul's teaching in 1 Corinthians 12, 13, and 14 is about God's love which speaks edification to the saints.

The purpose of utterance

Paul gave a beautiful summary of the purpose of utterance:

> 26. How is it then, brethren? when ye come together, every one of you hath a psalm, hath a doctrine, hath a tongue, hath a revelation, hath an interpretation. Let all things be done unto edifying.
> 1 Corinthians 14:26

"All things" in "let all things be done unto edifying" refers to psalm, doctrine, a tongue, a revelation, and an interpretation. These are all communicated via utterance, and they are to be done unto edification.

Recall that he had said:
> 3. But he that prophesieth speaketh unto men **TO** edification, and exhortation, and comfort.
> 1 Corinthians 14:3

The effect of prophesying is edification, which is expressed as exhortation, and comfort. The edification, exhortation, and comfort are the same. Not three separate things. So when Paul stated that prophecy comforts and exhorts, he was describing edification.

Thus, in 1 Corinthians 14:26, when Paul supposed that "all these things" (psalm, doctrine, a tongue, a revelation, and an interpretation) were to be done unto edification, he was also saying that any of psalm, doctrine, a tongue, a revelation, and an interpretation will comfort and exhort to edify.

This understanding that edification, exhortation, and comfort are the same and not three things helps unify our understanding of Paul's teaching in 1 Corinthians 14.

Why utterance?

31. For ye may all prophesy one by one, that all may learn, and
all may be comforted.
1 Corinthians 14:31

The Greek word translated "that" in "ye may all prophesy one by one, that all may learn" is **hina**, which is a word better translated as "so that". Prophecies are given so that "all may learn, and all may be comforted".

The Greek word **kai** translated as "and" in "all may learn, and all may be comforted" can be an explaining word or a connecting word. In this case, the text can also be read as "all may learn, which is to say all may be comforted". The "and" is an explaining word. "All may be comforted" is what Paul meant when he said, "all may learn".

All utterance should be done for the audience to learn or to be comforted. Given that edification, exhortation and comfort are the same and not three things, Paul has edification in mind when he states, "all may be comforted".

1 Corinthians 14:31, can then be restated as "all may learn, and all may be edified".

Paul explained the reason for utterance using the expression "by my voice":
18. I thank my God, I speak with tongues more than ye all:
19. Yet in the church I had rather speak five words with my understanding, that **BY MY VOICE** I might teach others also, than ten thousand words in an **UNKNOWN** tongue.
1 Corinthians 14:18-19

The Greek word translated "that" in "that by my voice I might teach others also" is **hina**, which is a word better translated as "so that". Paul spoke in his understanding to teach others.

Furthermore, the expression "by my voice" is in italics, meaning it was not in the original text.

Paul explained the purpose of utterance to be "I might teach others also". The Greek word translated "teach" means "to inform orally". In other words, speaking few words "with my understanding" informs others, while speaking "ten thousand words in an unknown tongue" cannot since men find it impossible to receive edification when they have not received understanding.

This point is illustrated further:
16. Else when thou shalt bless with the spirit, how shall he that occupieth the room of the unlearned say Amen at thy giving of thanks, seeing he understandeth not what thou sayest?
1 Corinthians 14:16

So here Paul explained "bless with the spirit" as "thy giving of thanks". Thus, "thou shalt bless with the spirit" is to give God thanks in tongues, since it is done in a language that the audience does not understand. This "he understandeth not what thou sayest" is why the hearer of the tongue which has not been accompanied with interpretation is called the unlearned in 1 Corinthians 14:16. In this verse, the unlearned is the audience who have heard the speaker in tongues but have not been given edification because the speaker in tongues has not given their minds the interpretation of the praise spoken to God in tongues.

This is happening in the church since there is an audience who are unable to "say Amen at thy giving of thanks". The responsibility of interpretation of the thanksgiving spoken to God in tongues sits with the speaker in tongues and not with the audience. The speaker in tongues, who is praising God in tongues is not carrying the audience along and might as well be at home speaking in private worship to God.

This reluctance of the speaker to walk in love towards the audience by giving them edification via understanding is what Paul had referred to as "I am become as sounding brass, or a tinkling cymbal" (see 1 Corinthians 13:1).

Is there something wrong with the tongues?

> 5. I would that ye all spake with tongues, but rather that ye prophesied: for greater **IS** he that prophesieth than he that speaketh with tongues, except he interpret, that the church may receive edifying.
> 1 Corinthians 14:5

Paul discusses tongues, interpretation, and prophecy together.

The Greek word translated "that" in "that the church may receive edifying" is **hina**, which means "so that". Paul's point is that the purpose or aim of tongues, interpretation, and prophecy is so that "the church may receive edifying".

Therefore, "ye all speak in tongues" refers to all those who are speaking a message to the church in tongues. The purpose or aim of such tongues addressed to the assembly, is not met until the church can receive edifying through interpretation. At the point that they receive understanding, prophecy has occurred.

This is Paul's explanation of his statement in the previous verse that "he that prophesieth edifieth the church" (see 1 Corinthians 14:4).

The correct understanding of Paul's teaching is that those who address the assembly in tongues must understand that they are doing so to arrive at prophecy.

Prophecy is speaking to men to edify them (see 1 Corinthians 14:3). Thus, prophecy in 1 Corinthians 14 is a short-hand way of speaking about the edification of the assembly through utterance.

Therefore, "ye all speak in tongues" is not addressed to every instance and scenario where the saints speak in tongues. It is not targeting the private expression of tongues as private devotion to God.

Paul's command that "he that speaketh with tongues should interpret it" is spoken in the context of "that the church may receive edifying". The setting of that instruction is the church receiving edification from tongues through its interpretation.

This is not so in private life.

> 4. He that speaketh in an **UNKNOWN** tongue edifieth himself; but he that prophesieth edifieth the church.
> 1 Corinthians 14:4

1 Corinthians 14:5 shows that the "prophesieth" in he that prophesieth edifieth the church" is that messages in tongues addressed to the assembly arrive at edifying through interpretation.

Observe that when Paul had said "He that speaketh in an unknown tongue edifieth himself", he did not include any instruction or command to interpret tongues in such cases. While, interpreting tongues in private devotion is not wrong, it is not commanded.

The principle of edification commands that uninterpreted tongues is inappropriate when it is addressed to the church.

Thus, prophecy is serving the assembly with interpreted tongues to edify them. Paul taught edification as being man to man or man to men. All supernatural manifestation in the assembly is subject to whether the church received edification or not. This means that Paul's "I would" is not a wish but the statement of a divine design.

> 17. For thou verily givest thanks well, but the other is not
> edified.
> 1 Corinthians 14:17

In the light of the edification principle, even praise spoken in uninterpreted tongues to the assembly has not hit the target if the church is not edified.

All thanksgiving in tongues is excellent communion between the speaker and God. Since edification is between men, excellent communion between God and man is not the same thing as excellent communion between brethren.

Praise being very good is one thing and edification in the assembly is another. The two are not the same thing. When a man gives thanks in tongues, it always meets the requirement of good worship. The same thanksgiving in tongues will fail the edification criteria unless interpreted.

Thus, I can give thanks in tongues very well, and yet my brother is not edified.

When Paul said, "thou verily givest thanks well", he is describing thanksgiving that the audience does not understand!

"Thou verily givest thanks well" means that although the unlearned do not understand it, the tongues is not faulty, fake, or non-genuine.

The fact is, the bible does not teach or attach the concept of fakery or non-genuineness to tongues. There are no tests for measuring the originality or absence of the same of tongues. The issue was not the authenticity of the tongues but the improper administration of tongues in that it was exercised as uninterpreted tongues which do not edify.

The edification principle is how we judge utterance. Nothing escapes or is higher than the principle of edification.

Why is the audience not edified? The people in the audience are not edified because they have minds. The mind is not edified by hearing the tongues. Edification is targeted at the mind, therefore it is a thing of understanding, which usually comes by interpretation of tongues.

The implication of all these is that while tongues is supernatural, given by the indwelling spirit and a sign of the gospel already believed, the act of giving a message to the assembly in tongues in and of itself does not edify the hearers of such tongues. Uninterpreted tongues carry no power of edification. There must be something added to the tongues for edification to happen in the understanding of the audience.

12. Even so ye, forasmuch as ye are zealous of spiritual
GIFTS, seek that ye may excel to the edifying of the church.
1 Corinthians 14:12

The word translated spiritual in "spiritual gifts" is the word
pneuma, which means spirit. It is a figure where the spirit is
used to refer to the parts or things given by the spirit.

The word translated "zealous" here means "to defend", "contend for", "be desirous of" or "uphold a thing". It is good to be
zealous of spiritual gifts.

The word translated "seek" means "to think" or "meditate on".

The word translated "excel" means "to exceed a fixed number
of measure", "to go above a number", "to overflow", or "to
exceed".

Put together, our God-given assignment is to meditate on our
administration of utterance so that we go above, overflow or
exceed on the matter of communicating the understanding of
that which has been addressed to men in tongues.

Whereas the saints tend to prioritise things like accuracy in
the exercise of spiritual gifts, the phonetics of the sound of
tongues, or the degree to which the audience is in awe of the
power on display, what Paul prioritised was consistency in edifying the church.

6. Now, brethren, if I come unto you speaking with tongues,
what shall I profit you, except I shall speak to you either by
revelation, or by knowledge, or by prophesying, or by doctrine?
1 Corinthians 14:6

The "you" in "I come unto you" are the brethren. The speaker
in tongues is coming to the brethren speaking with tongues.
Since the speaker is addressing the audience, this is no longer

between the speaker and God. It is between the speaker and the audience. There is nothing wrong with starting our message to the church in tongues but the act of coming as a messenger speaking to the people in tongues is not what profits the audience. The edification comes via the revelation, knowledge, prophesying, or doctrine spoken in the understanding to the people who had initially heard what had been spoken in tongues.

Starting our message to the church in tongues is the first step but it is by no means the final. "Profit" is not in being bold enough to address the message to the church in tongues. It is whether I used my utterance to edify or not. The edification principle means the speaker in tongues asks "did I discharge the duty of the messenger, which is to give understanding or not?". This way, edification regulates the efficacy of utterance.

Thou hast had five husbands

16. Jesus saith unto her, Go, call thy husband, and come hither.
17. The woman answered and said, I have no husband. Jesus said unto her, Thou hast well said, I have no husband: 18. For thou hast had five husbands; and he whom thou now hast is not thy husband: in that saidst thou truly. 19. The woman saith unto him, Sir, I perceive that thou art a prophet. 20. Our fathers worshipped in this mountain; and ye say, that in Jerusalem is the place where men ought to worship. 21. Jesus saith unto her, Woman, believe me, the hour cometh, when ye shall neither in this mountain, nor yet at Jerusalem, worship the Father.
John 4:16-21

Jesus gave a word of knowledge which He conveyed in the words, "For thou hast had five husbands; and he whom thou now hast is not thy husband: in that saidst thou truly".

We know He was very accurate because the woman replied, "Sir,

I perceive that thou art a prophet". Since she recognized Jesus as a prophet, we know that Jesus had her attention.

Observe that John's emphasis in the passage was not to make us know how many husbands she had been married to. Jesus' ministry to that woman could not have been to inform her of the number of husbands that she had had – she already knew that! He mentioned her five husbands to get her attention so He could minister to her.

Jesus started with her relationships but did not stay there. He got her attention to take her mind away from her relational woes into a comprehension of Christ. Likewise, it is what we do with that attention that we refer to as edification or the lack of.

28. The woman then left her waterpot, and went her way into the city, and saith to the men, 29. Come, see a man, which told me all things that ever I did: is not this the Christ?
John 4:28-29

We see the impact of Jesus' ministry in that this woman went to preach to others the revelation of Jesus.

Tell the vision to no man

1. And after six days Jesus taketh Peter, James, and John his brother, and bringeth them up into an high mountain apart, 2. And was transfigured before them: and his face did shine as the sun, and his raiment was white as the light. 3. And, behold, there appeared unto them Moses and Elias talking with him. 4. Then answered Peter, and said unto Jesus, Lord, it is good for us to be here: if thou wilt, let us make here three tabernacles; one for thee, and one for Moses, and one for Elias. 5. While he yet spake, behold, a bright cloud overshadowed them: and behold a voice out of the cloud, which said, This is my

beloved Son, in whom I am well pleased; hear ye him. 6. And
when the disciples heard IT, they fell on their face, and were
sore afraid. 7. And Jesus came and touched them, and said,
Arise, and be not afraid. 8. And when they had lifted up their
eyes, they saw no man, save Jesus only.

Matthew 17:1-8

Jesus took Peter, James, and John up a physical mountain to
pray. While Jesus prayed, He was transfigured before His disciples. This transfiguration was genuine, supernatural, and of
God.

During this event on the mountain, the disciples heard God say,
"This is my beloved Son, in whom I am well pleased; hear ye
him". Before hearing God, Peter had told Jesus, "it is good for
us to be here: if thou wilt, let us make here three tabernacles;
one for thee, and one for Moses, and one for Elias". Incredibly,
in that atmosphere where the glory of God was tangible, Peter's
thought was on the building of tabernacles.

It was while Peter communicated his understanding about the
building of tabernacles that God said, "This is my beloved Son,
in whom I am well pleased; hear ye him".

In other words, Peter was to keep quiet, listen to Jesus and learn.
However, Peter had other ideas which he spoke out.

The bright cloud that overshadowed them while Peter spoke
was not a validation of Peter or of Peter's words about the disciples entering into a tabernacle-building programme. The fact
that the bright cloud appeared when Peter spoke was to draw
Peter away from his conclusions.

9. And as they came down from the mountain, Jesus charged
them, saying, Tell the vision to no man, until the Son of man
be risen again from the dead.

Matthew 17:9

Since Jesus said, "tell the vision to no man", He acknowledged that Peter had seen a vision. More importantly, He concluded that Peter's understanding of a temple-building programme was not to be repeated to anyone else. It failed the edification test. Jesus' command to tell the vision to no man shows that Peter's seeing a vision is not equivalent to understanding what to do with the vision or the message conveyed in the vision. By implication, there is more maturity required in the retelling of visions than in seeing the visions in the first place. This is true whether this is a bona fide vision or a fluke.

What were they to wait for before telling the vision?

They were to wait for the resurrection. In the resurrection, they would receive understanding from which they would believe and preach the message of the gospel. In the light of the resurrection, they would know what to emphasize in retelling the vision to people. They were not to tell it until they had a revelation of the resurrection. It is in the truth of the resurrection that we understand where to place our emphasis.

We know that seeing the vision is not the big deal because, in this Matthew 17 transfiguration story, before Peter, James, and John received eternal life, they saw in a vision accurately.

Equally, before Cornelius received eternal life, he saw in a vision accurately (see Acts 10:3), and after Paul had received eternal life, he saw in a vision accurately (see Acts 22:17-21). So, anyone can see a vision, but seeing accurately and saying accurately is not the same thing. Retelling accurately requires discipleship.

A vision can be genuine, accurate, and precise yet what is ministered through it by the one who has seen the vision is not edifying. Supernatural experiences are not in themselves edification, but they are a bona fide way of grabbing the attention of men.

Edification through spoken words

Paul's emphasis in 1 Corinthians 14 shows that among believers, edification will come through the spoken words from men to men.

> 26. How is it then, brethren? when ye come together, every one of you hath a psalm, hath a doctrine, hath a tongue, hath a revelation, hath an interpretation. Let all things be done unto edifying.
> 1 Corinthians 14:26

The "all things" to be done unto edifying are the giving of the psalm, doctrine, tongues, revelation, and interpretation. Addressing the saints in tongues and interpretation is to be done unto edifying. Since "all things" are to be administered with edification in mind, when utterance is given but the saints are not edified, the utterance has failed the edification test.

Paul made this point using different words:

> 40. Let all things be done decently and in order.
> 1 Corinthians 14:40

The "all things" refer to prophesying and speaking in tongues which had been mentioned in the previous verse – "Wherefore, brethren, covet to prophesy, and forbid not to speak with tongues" (see 1 Corinthians 14:39).

The word translated "decently" describes our conduct towards others. Since Paul is writing about bringing profit or edification unto others, "decently" is the conduct of seeing to it that we edify and not just speak in tongues in addressing the congregation. The word translated "order" describes how things are arranged. It is doing things the right way.

What order is Paul referring to?

> 39. Wherefore, brethren, covet to prophesy, and forbid not to
> speak with tongues.
> 1 Corinthians 14:39

These are Paul's concluding words to his arguments in 1 Corinthians 12, 13, and 14.

The words "covet earnestly" in 1 Corinthians 12:31, is the same word translated as "desire" in 1 Corinthians 14:1 and "covet" in 1 Corinthians 14:39. This shows that Paul continued a singular argument to covet to prophesy in 1 Corinthians 12, 13, and 14.

The saint who will prophesy will not forbid speaking with tongues, because speaking in tongues is a valid way to arrive at prophecy. Prophesying is Paul's summary of his teaching on the edification of others. When it comes to the assembly, the saint is not to see speaking in tongues as an end but the door into edifying the saints.

What is the order that follows tongues?

> 5. I would that ye all spake with tongues, but rather that ye
> prophesied: for greater **IS** he that prophesieth than he that
> speaketh with tongues, except he interpret, that the church
> may receive edifying.
> 1 Corinthians 14:5

Prophecy is speaking edification to the church (14:3).

The Greek word translated "that" is a word better translated as "so that".

In the church, Paul wanted the saints to use tongues to address the church so that the speaker in tongues may prophesy. The intent of addressing the church in tongues is to arrive at prophecy, which is the edification of the church via the interpretation of tongues. Thus, the scriptural order that produces edification to the church is that interpretation of tongues after speaking in tongues. Uninterpreted tongues is disorder in that the assembly won't be edified.

The terms "decently" and "order" describe the same thing. Paul is reminding the saints that the right actions that accompany tongues are those that lead to edification.

Observe the following:

> 31. For ye may all prophesy one by one, that all may learn, and all may be comforted.
> 1 Corinthians 14:31

The edification principle causes us to treat prophecy as interpreted tongues. Thus, we can render verse 31 as "For ye may all speak in tongues and follow it up with interpretation one by one, that all may learn, and all may be comforted."

The word translated "learn" in "that all may learn" is **manthano**, which means "to increase one's knowledge", which is discipleship. Since learning is involved in receiving edification, it means that a foundation of discipleship is the best foundation for profiting from utterance. If a man given to God's word gives us an utterance, we harvest his words best by being given to the written word ourselves.

Your knowledge of God's word affects what you pay attention to in utterance and how you listen to and receive from what you are hearing. A person who doesn't give much attention to the written word would likely not listen properly to words spoken as utterance.

Speaking in utterance to an audience presupposes that the audience is given to the written word. The things spoken as utterances are not an alternative to the written word but are instead governed by it. Our utterances would agree with the written word.

Utterance is of optimal impact when the hearers are disciples who prioritise the word. Such people can do a lot with little utterance.

The student of the word will do a better job when giving utterance and the hearers who are students of the word will do a better job receiving what has been spoken. This is because the knowledge of God's word has a purifying effect on the minds of both the speaker and hearers.

A student of the word will do more with the words spoken in utterance than the saint who does not pay attention to the written word. However, if the speaker in tongues is full of the word but the hearts of the hearers were dull, the power of edification communicated is diminished by the dullness of the minds of the hearers.

Thus, edification is maximized when both the speaker in prophecy (tongues followed by interpretation) and the one receiving the words of prophecy are both students of the word. You see, the word is so powerful that the understanding of the word improves both the speaker and the hearer.

As we grow spiritually by giving our minds to God's word, we draw more insights from the same statements we had heard before, because the written word brings clarity to our minds. It is often mind-boggling what we hear when we listen again to an utterance that had been spoken to us when we were much younger in the faith. We would likely be shocked by what had been said in comparison to what we had understood as younger believers.

In our spiritual growth, by the word we have the spiritual understanding which causes us to observe things in a better way.

As we grow, we pay attention more correctly to spiritual things, for we'll be taking note of the important things. The change in emphasis unlocks our minds to see more clearly and correctly.

As the speaker in tongues gives attention to God's word, the word strips away immature thinking. It is not the tongues that needs to become "stronger". It is the understanding that needs to be trained in the word, and this, in turn, changes effectiveness in utterance.

The edification principle means that since "ye may all prophesy one by one, that all may learn", we should spend even more time following the administration of the interpretation of tongues with a clearer explanation of the things emphasized in the interpretation of tongues. When we explain more, the hearers get past the initial excitement of hearing an utterance and learn to dwell on the contents of the message given and its implications.

How you listen to a prophecy determines the quality of edification you'd receive from it.

There is an excitement that goes with the supernatural. This excitement is not evil but it is not to be confused with or mistaken from understanding.

8

TONGUES OF MEN AND OF ANGELS

1. Though I speak with the tongues of men and of angels, and
have not charity, I am become **AS** sounding brass, or a tinkling
cymbal.
1 Corinthians 13:1

The "tongues" that Paul refers to in "though I speak with
the tongues of men and of angels" is his explanation of
what he had referred to as "the divers kinds of tongues"
in 1 Corinthians 12:10.

The tongue of angels?

What did Paul mean by "angel" in "tongues of angels? Had Paul
switched to talking to men about angelic beings or is he continuing his correction from 1 Corinthians 12 and thus discussing
how men minister to other men?

In our western minds, the word "angel" elicits the imagery of
angelic beings. That is sometimes correct, but is it always the
case in the text of scripture?

The Greek word translated as "angels" is **Angelos,** a word that means messenger or envoy. One who comes with or bears a message. To understand what Paul meant by the word that has been translated as angel here, we do well to consider the use of the word in scriptures.

How did the writers of the synoptic gospels, who were either the students of the apostles or the apostles themselves use the word "angel"?

Whereas the word **Angelos** is indeed used to refer to angelic beings, that is not the only use of the term:

7. And as they departed, Jesus began to say unto the multitudes concerning John, What went ye out into the wilderness to see? A reed shaken with the wind? 8. But what went ye out for to see? A man clothed in soft raiment? behold, they that wear soft **CLOTHING** are in kings' houses. 9. But what went ye out for to see? A prophet? yea, I say unto you, and more than a prophet. 10. For this is HE, of whom it is written, Behold, I send my messenger before thy face, which shall prepare thy way before thee.
Matthew 11:7-10

Jesus refers to John as "my messenger". The Greek word translated "messenger" is the word **angelos,** which is the word usually translated as angel. Here, Jesus referred to John as an angel.

52. And sent messengers before his face: and they went, and entered into a village of the Samaritans, to make ready for him.
Luke 9:52

The Greek word translated "messengers" is the word **angelos,** which is angels. Luke calls the men that Jesus sent to the village of the Samaritans, angels.

24. And when the messengers of John were departed, he
began to speak unto the people concerning John, What went
ye out into the wilderness for to see? A reed shaken with the
wind?

Luke 7:24

Again, the Greek word translated "messengers" is the word **angelos**, which is angels. Luke calls the disciples of John, angels.

Some uses of the word "angel" in Acts and the epistles

For example, Paul used that word this way:

13. Ye know how through infirmity of the flesh I preached the
gospel unto you at the first. 14. And my temptation which was
in my flesh ye despised not, nor rejected; but received me as an
angel of God, **EVEN** as Christ Jesus.

Galatians 4:13-14

Paul, the preacher to the Galatians reminds them that they had
not despised him on account of his infirmities. When he came
to them, they had received him as an angel of God. He did not
mean that he became of the class of spirit beings called angels.
He meant that the Galatians had received him as a messenger of
God. Receiving a man as a messenger of God is far higher than
receiving the man as belonging to the angelic class of beings.

Paul was the messenger or message-bearing one, who had come
with the gospel message to the churches of Galatia. This made
him the angel of the church of Galatians.

This sheds light on his earlier use of "angel" in Galatians 1.

9. As we said before, so say I now again, If any **MAN** preach
any other gospel unto you than that ye have received, let him

be accursed.

Galatians 1:9

He said, "as we said before so say I now again". Paul means that he is repeating himself for emphasis.

What he said is "if any man preach any other gospel unto you".

Who do we receive ministry from? We receive this ministry from those men who preach to us.

This fact concerning when to receive or not receive ministry from men would be what he had said before – and it is what he was repeating. So let us examine the previous verse.

> 8. But though we, or an angel from heaven, preach any other gospel unto you than that which we have preached unto you, let him be accursed.
>
> Galatians 1:8

He said, "though we or an angel from heaven preach". In Greek, the word translated as angel simply means messenger. Who are the preachers? They are men. Paul's "we" would be himself and others who preached the gospel to the Galatians.

He restated in verse 9 the very point that he had made in verse 8, using two different words to convey the same argument – he said, "we or an angel from heaven". "We" and "angel from heaven" refer to preachers of the gospel. He was not talking about angelic beings.

This point about men is clearer in Galatians 1:9 where Paul affirmed that he was repeating his earlier point and not making a new one without using the term angels.

Thus, when Paul had said, "though we or an angel from heaven", he was not referring two different things but one. He used the term "angel from heaven" to clarify that these men are messengers of God who had brought the gospel or the good news of God to men.

Here is another example of Paul's use of the term angel:

16. And without controversy great is the mystery of godliness: God was manifest in the flesh, justified in the Spirit, seen of angels, preached unto the Gentiles, believed on in the world, received up into glory.

1 Timothy 3:16

In His resurrection, Jesus is seen of angels, who preached Him unto Gentiles.

Who were these angels that saw Jesus in His resurrection?

4. And that he was buried, and that he rose again the third day according to the scriptures: 5. And that he was seen of Cephas, then of the twelve:

1 Corinthians 15:4-5

After Jesus "rose again the third day", He was seen of Cephas and then of the twelve. Both Cephas and the twelve are preachers. It
Is these preachers that saw Jesus after His resurrection who Paul referred to as angels.

Thus, in 1 Timothy 3:16, the angels who saw Jesus in the resurrection and preached Him among the gentiles were men who went everywhere with the gospel.

What was the message of these angels (or messengers)?

21. Wherefore of these men which have companied with us all the time that the Lord Jesus went in and out among us, 22. Beginning from the baptism of John, unto that same day that he was taken up from us, must one be ordained to be a witness

with us of his resurrection.
Acts 1:21-22

According to Peter, the apostles, who are the angels that saw
Jesus after His resurrection were to be witnesses of the resurrection.

1. And as they spake unto the people, the priests, and the
captain of the temple, and the Sadducees, came upon them,
2. Being grieved that they taught the people, and preached
through Jesus the resurrection from the dead.
Acts 4:1-2

The apostles "preached through Jesus the resurrection from the
dead". The message of these angels who saw Jesus after His
resurrection was the resurrection that they had seen as the fulfilment of the scriptures.

25. Likewise also was not Rahab the harlot justified by works,
when she had received the messengers, and had sent THEM
out another way?
James 2:25

Yet again, the Greek word translated "messengers" is the word
angelos. So James calls the twelve spies that the Lord had told
Moses to send into Canaan in Numbers 13, angels. Again, we
observe that these angels that James spoke of are men.

The angel of the churches

1. Unto the angel of the church of Ephesus write; These
things saith he that holdeth the seven stars in his right hand,
who walketh in the midst of the seven golden candlesticks;
Revelation 2:1

Jesus commanded John to write a letter to seven churches, documented in the book of Revelation. Was Jesus telling John to write a physical scroll to be delivered to celestial beings (angels), who in turn would read these letters to the saints?

What would the leaders of the saints have been doing while all these were happing?

We have seen that John, a prophet was called an angel and that Paul, an apostle, referred to himself as an angel to the Galatians. Therefore, the angels of the seven churches would be those preachers who bring the word of God to them.

It is likely the seven churches sent these angels to John and John's letters would have been sent through these angels, who would have then read and explained them to each of the seven churches.

We see that in each church (see Revelations 2-3), made up of men, John addressed his letter to the angel of the church, which would have been the elders or ministers who bring doctrine to the saints.

Therefore, "angel" could refer to men or celestial beings. Only by examining the context can we determine whether it refers to spirit beings or human messengers.

13. Ye know how through infirmity of the flesh I preached the gospel unto you at the first. 14. And my temptation which was in my flesh ye despised not, nor rejected; but received me as an angel of God, EVEN as Christ Jesus.
Galatians 4:13-14

We know that the word translated "angel" here refers to men and not to angelic beings because Paul was speaking of himself as a preacher of the gospel who had been honoured by being received as one with the message of the almighty God.

Although the Bible speaks of a distinct race of spirit beings who are not men but angelic beings, there's so much material on Paul that confirms that he was a man and not an angelic being. It is as a preacher that he referred to himself as an angel of God.

Does Paul teach about angelic tongues?

1. Though I speak with the tongues of men and of angels, and have not charity, I am become AS sounding brass, or a tinkling cymbal.

1 Corinthians 13:1

We know these:

Jesus called John, a preacher who preached God's word to men, an angel; James also called the twelve spies who came back with a report, angels; Paul too, referred to himself as an angel to the Galatians; both John's (the Baptist) and Jesus' disciples were called angels; and John the apostle referred to the elders of the churches as angels. Therefore, it follows that Paul's "angels" in "tongues of men and of angels" are men who are messengers in the Corinthian church.

When Paul said to the Corinthians, "though I speak with the tongues of men and of angels", he meant "I am a messenger using tongues to address my message to you". His further statement, "I speak with the tongues of angels", meant that he was not using tongues in a devotional way, in which case it would have been between the speaker in tongues and God. He meant that the saints could use tongues to convey a message for the benefit of the other saints gathered in the church.

Speaking in tongues of angels is speaking in tongues not as a prayer or communion with God but as a messenger to the assembly.

More importantly, Paul's term "I speak with the tongues of angels" did not mean angelic and non-angelic tongues as a variety of tongues. The tendency to think of varieties to tongue is due to a misunderstanding of 1 Corinthians 12:10.

> 10. To another the working of miracles; to another prophecy; to another discerning of spirits; to another **DIVERS** kinds of tongues; to another the interpretation of tongues:
> 1 Corinthians 12:10

The word "divers" is in italics because there is no such word in the Greek text. The verse correctly reads "kinds of tongues". The Greek word translated "kinds" is **genos**, meaning "of a particular nation", "of a family", "of a tribe or a people". So, as explained earlier, diverse kinds of tongues is the vocal ability of the household of faith, or the household of God. It is the tongue associated with a distinct people whose faith in the resurrection differentiates them from all others. It is spirit-given vocal ability. There is only one kind of it, the type given by the spirit.

The saint does not get born again so that the indwelling spirit can finally grant the saint the linguistics of angels. That would be a demotion since angels who apparently must speak angel language do not need to be born again to gain such powers.

Moreover, in all the epistles there is no single instance of an angel speaking in tongues. Angels cannot speak kinds of tongues since it is a vocal ability from the indwelling of God's spirit.

More specifically, in Paul's letter to the Corinthians, it is always the saints that do the speaking in tongues.

For example:

"Though I speak with the tongues of men and of angels" (1

Cor 13:1).

The saint does the speaking.

"For he that speaketh in an unknown tongue" (1 Corinthians 14:2).

The saint is the "he" that is doing the speaking.

"He that speaketh in an unknown tongue" (1 Corinthians 14:4).

The saint is the "he" that is doing the speaking.

"I would that ye all spake with tongues" (1 Corinthians 14:5) Paul is instructing men and not angels. The saints are the "ye all" that are doing the speaking.

"He that speaketh with tongues" (1 Corinthians 14:5).

The saint is the "he" that is doing the speaking.

"If I come unto you speaking with tongues" (1 Corinthians 14:6).

Paul is the "I" that is doing the speaking.

"Let him that speaketh in an unknown tongue" (1 Corinthians 14:13).

This "him", is the saint that is doing the speaking.

"If I pray in an unknown tongue" (1 Corinthians 14:14).

Paul is the "I" that is doing the speaking.

"I speak with tongues more than ye all" (1 Corinthians 14:18).

Paul is the "I" that is doing the speaking.

"If any man speak in an unknown tongue" (1 Corinthians 14:27).

Again, men are the ones doing the speaking.

What we find in Paul's Corinthian epistle is that it is never the angelic beings that speak in tongues. What Paul said was "though I speak with the tongues of men and of angels". The I in "I speak" is Paul, a man.

"I speak" means that Paul, who is human and not angelic, is the speaker in tongues. So, Paul's term "I speak with the tongues of men and of angels" is not promoting the idea that angelic communication is some higher mode of communication that angelic beings use to instruct the saints or some form of tongues that men use to try to mimic angels.

In the scriptures, the saint is never told to mimic angelic beings. There is nothing for the saint to gain doing that. If anything, the reverse is true – the saint is the educator of the angels.

> 1. Be ye therefore followers of God, as dear children;
> Ephesians 5:1

The saint is a follower or imitator of God because the saint is a dear child of God.

The term "I speak with the tongues of men and of angels" means that God is not the audience of such speaking in tongues; rather men are. It is speaking as one with a message for an audience speaking with the aim of edifying men, but beginning the communication in tongues.

Therefore, the term "angel" in "I speak with the tongues of men and of angels" is not a reference to angels like Gabriel or

Michael.

So where does "I speak with the tongues of men and of angels" take place in Paul's writings?

> 5. I would that ye all spake with tongues, but rather that ye prophesied: for greater **IS** he that prophesieth than he that speaketh with tongues, except he interpret, that the church may receive edifying.
> 1 Corinthians 14:5

This speaker in tongues is doing so in the church intending to convey a message to the church therefore this is speaking in tongues as a messenger to the church, which is what is called tongues of angels. The setting for speaking in tongues as a messenger or angel is the church, the same setting for all the instructions in 1 Corinthians 12, 13, and 14 is the church (see 1 Corinthians 14:12, 19, 23, 26, 28, 33). If others were not present, there would be no need to speak of the importance of charity.

Charity is love. Love in the epistles, and as seen in Christ, is directed towards others.

If such speaking in tongues does not result in the church receiving edifying, the speaker in tongues has spoken with "the tongues of men and of angels, and have not charity" (see 1 Corinthians 13:1).

> 1. Though I speak with the tongues of men and of angels, and have not charity, I am become **AS** sounding brass, or a tinkling cymbal.
> 1 Corinthians 13:1

The word "of" in both "of angels" or "of men" is not in Greek. It was added by translators to make it more readable in English. Therefore, a closer rendition of the Greek is "though I speak with the tongues men and angels"

The Greek word that has been translated "and" in "I speak with the tongues of men and of angels" is a word that could be explanatory or a word that joins different ideas. Here, the subject matter is tongues. The "and" is explanatory.

Paul was simply saying, "Though I speak with the tongues of men which are angels or message carriers,". These are men speaking as messengers.

Paul used the terms "sounding brass and tinkling cymbal" in explaining the effect of speaking with the tongues of men and of angels on the audience. Paul has not suddenly become an instructor on musical instruments. Rather, he was only employing the imagery of musical instruments. "Sounding brass and tinkling cymbal" means that there are instruments to be seen but there is no meaningful music coming forth. The musical harmony that the instruments are capable of is not realized.

The intent of the imagery was the question was "although the assembly can hear the sound of tongues coming from the speaker in tongues, is it having the intended effect of edifying the audience?"

"Sounding brass and tinkling cymbal" was Paul's way of saying that the while the audience may have seen and heard the speaker in tongues not much that was useful to the audience may have been happening. Sounds are being voiced out just for the sake of sounds without meeting the goal of the edification of the audience. So, when tongues is uninterpreted, it is called "have not charity".

In other words, I, for instance, may have addressed the saints as an angel (one with a message) without delivering the message. They have heard me say things in tongues, but the audience may not have understood what I said. Such a messenger is failing to show his or her love for the saints in the audience. Love would instead edify them with the interpretation of tongues.

By speaking in tongues to the brethren without taking them beyond hearing tongues, I have the appearance of one who has served. However, I have not really served because the minds of my audience have no idea what I have saying.

It is possible to speak in tongues as someone with a message and have not love (have not the edification of the hearers of the tongues in mind). This should not be the case, yet it happens. Paul gave some instructions on the proper use of utterance to serve edification to the church.

"I am become as sounding brass, or a tinkling cymbal" means I am not doing love's job of edification of those who heard the tongues.

Thus, 1 Corinthians 13:1 is Paul's statement of the problem in Corinth. Notice that he does not merely state the problem and stop there – love would not do that. Love would point out the issue with the view to state the answer. Thus, Paul points out how to remedy the "sounding brass, or a tinkling cymbal" problem.

The remedy is given here:

1. Follow after charity, and desire spiritual **GIFTS**, but rather that ye may prophesy.
1 Corinthians 14:1

Paul's answer to "have not love" in 1 Corinthians 13:1 is to "follow after charity". This term "follow after charity", shows that the believer already possesses the love of God. The question is "is he or she guided by that love?".

This command to "follow after charity" shows that when Paul had said earlier in 1 Corinthians 13:1 "have not love", he did not mean that the saint was without God's love. He was only saying that the speaker in tongues was not using the knowledge of God's love already received in the gospel, to guide his or her utterance to other saints to edify them.

Since charity is serving others to edify them, the term "follow after charity" means aim for the edification of others.

This means that Paul's teaching about utterance in 1 Corinthians 14 was about the love walk of the believer as a consequence of God's love.

9

GREATER

Paul gave a brilliant illustration of prophecy as the pursuit of love in 1 Corinthians 14:5.

5. I would that ye all spake with tongues, but rather that ye prophesied: for greater **IS** he that prophesieth than he that speaketh with tongues, except he interpret, that the church may receive edifying.
1 Corinthians 14:5

This is the key verse that captures Paul's meaning in his 1 Corinthians 12,13 and 14 discuss.

> **"** *Interpretation of tongues is the bridge between tongues and edification.* **"**

Let's consider Paul's "I would that ye all spake with tongues, but rather that ye prophesied".

Prophecy is speaking to men to edify them (see 1 Corinthians 14:3).

Ye in "ye all spake with tongues" is an old English plural pronoun that means all of you.

The word "Ye" in "ye all spake with tongues" is an old English plural pronoun that means "all of you". Since prophecy

> **It is a scriptural journey from tongues until the destination which is edification.**

is speaking to the church, when Paul said "ye all spake with tongues", he was addressing all that use tongues to address the church. These are vital instructions for the other speaker in the church, whom he commanded "let him keep silence in the church; and let him speak to himself, and to God" (see 1 Corinthians 14:28), for such a person was not speaking to the church to bring forth edification.

So the "ye all speak in tongues" refers to all who had a message to speak to the church, including all those who were keeping silent in the church because there had been no interpretation.

That expression "but rather" means "most especially".

The Greek word translated "that" in "but rather that ye prophesied" is **hina**, which is a word better translated as "so that".

A loose translation of the sentence is "I would all of you that use tongues to address the church do so most especially so that ye prophesied".

Thus, Paul was saying those that had something to say to the church, and who attempted to do so in tongues must understand that they were doing so to arrive at prophecy. He was advocating for speaking in tongues in the assembly with the aim of prophecy. His "I would" was not a wish but the statement of a divine design.

Therefore, the intent behind addressing the church in tongues is to arrive at prophecy which is the giving of the meaning of the tongues to the audience.

The answer to the problem that had been stated in 1 Corinthians 13:1 is introduced in 1 Corinthians 14:1 and described in great detail in 1 Corinthians 14:5.

The Greek word translated "that" in "that the church may receive edifying" is **hina**, which is a word better translated as "so that". Thus, Paul was teaching about the purpose of prophecy. When anyone prophesies it is so that "all may learn, and all may be comforted".

> *Interpretation of tongues is how the riches possessed in tongues are given to be received by the minds of the audience.*

Paul demonstrated that the divine design in all such use of utterance, whether tongues or the interpretation of it was "that the church may receive edifying".

What is the church receiving?

5. I would that ye all spake with tongues, but rather that ye prophesied: for greater **IS** he that prophesieth than he that speaketh with tongues, except he interpret, that the church may receive edifying.
1 Corinthians 14:5

Since Paul taught about "he that speaketh with tongues", the text in 1 Corinthians 14:2 was a backdrop for understanding what Paul has written in 1 Corinthians 14:5.

2. For he that speaketh in an **UNKNOWN** tongue speaketh not unto men, but unto God: for no man understandeth **HIM**; howbeit in the spirit he speaketh mysteries.
1 Corinthians 14:2

Paul described speaking in tongues as he "speaketh not unto men" because "no man understandeth him". The "him" in "no man understandeth him" is italicized. There is no "him" there in the original Greek text. So, it was not "him" that is not understood by the minds of the audience, but the tongues that were not understood.

The speaker in tongues can be said to be speaking "unto God" because until interpreted to give understanding to the audience, the things said in tongues are unknown to the minds of the people that have heard the tongues. Such use of tongues would be devotional, directed at God.

Paul picks up on this in verse 9:

> 9. So likewise ye, except ye utter by the tongue words easy to be understood, how shall it be known what is spoken? for ye shall speak into the air.
> 1 Corinthians 14:9

The Greek word that has been translated "utter" in "except ye utter by the tongue words" is **didomi**, which means to give something to someone. To "utter by the tongue" means to give something to someone by words.

What is being uttered by the tongue? The thing that is being given by the speaker to the audience is words that are easy to be understood. The thing that is to be given, which would be easy to understand, cannot be tongues, for "he that speaketh in an unknown tongue speaketh not unto men, but unto God: for no man understandeth him" (see 1 Corinthians 14:2).

> 7. And even things without life giving sound, whether pipe or harp, except they give a distinction in the sounds, how shall it be known what is piped or harped? 8. For if the trumpet give an uncertain sound, who shall prepare himself to the battle? 9. So likewise ye, except ye utter by the tongue words easy to be understood, how shall it be known what is spoken? for ye shall speak into the air. 10. There are, it may be, so many kinds of voices in the world, and none of them **IS** without signification.
> 1 Corinthians 14:7-10

In his explanation, Paul mentioned inanimate things like pipe or harp, but his subject matter was neither. Then he mentioned trumpets that give an uncertain, indistinct, or obscure sound. The word translated "uncertain" means a hidden sound.

His expression "so likewise ye" shows that his reference to pipe, harp, or trumpet was a figure for the message spoken by saints. Paul only used the imagery of the sounding of trumpets in the bible.

> It is the love-duty of the speaker in tongues to supply the interpretation to the audience.

When Paul spoke of the sounding of the trumpet, he was referring to the sounds (tongues) from the mouths of the saints. The sound of the trumpet penetrates the mind and ushers the saints into edification. We must understand that Paul was using metaphors to explain tongues.

If one speaks in tongues without interpretation, it is the same thing as the trumpet not giving a clear sound. Thus, the audience does not understand what the trumpet (the message) is saying.

The speaking forth of revelation, knowledge, prophesying, or doctrine is the trumpet giving a certain sound. This intent of the sounding of the trumpet (speaking utterance in the assembly) is to gather the saints unto edification.

The student of the word will notice that in the KJV, every time we see that expression "unknown tongue" in 1 Corinthians 14, "unknown" is italicized. Paul never wrote about unknown tongues.

Paul's point rather was that though the audience had heard tongues, there was something yet to be given.

The context was that although the audience hears the words spoken in tongues, those words were not easy to be understood by the minds of the audience because simply listening to tongues did not give understanding. Something needed to be given in addition for the saints understanding.

Hearing tongues leaves the hearer needing a revelation of what has been said. It is this revelation that gives understanding. Without this revelation of what has been said in tongues, Paul asked "how shall it be known what is spoken?".

"How shall it be known what is spoken?" means something has been spoken but no knowledge has been uttered or given to the hearers. The hearers are none the better.

Now the word "receive" in "that the church may receive edifying" is **lambano**, meaning "to seize" or "take". The edification belongs to the saints but the saints cannot seize it without the speaker in tongues ministering the edification via interpretation of tongues.

So Paul instructed the speaker in tongues to prioritize giving the audience the interpretation, rather than leaving it to them to figure out. Instead, it is the love-duty of the speaker in tongues to supply the interpretation to the audience.

The speaker who addresses the audience in tongues has spoken unto God in devotion and not unto man (verse 2), which in verse 9 is described as "ye shall speak into the air" in that the audience doesn't understand. This is because the audience of tongues is not the mind of men. Something has to be given in addition to tongues for men to become the audience.

Do the "greater"

5. I would that ye all spake with tongues, but rather that ye
prophesied: for greater **IS** he that prophesieth than he that
speaketh with tongues, except he interpret, that the church
may receive edifying.
1 Corinthians 14:5

Given Paul's explanation in verses 2 and 9, the things spoken
by "he that speaketh with tongues" are not understood by the
church just because the church heard the tongues. While the
speaker in tongues is edified by speaking, the audience is not.

Observe the expression "he that speaketh with tongues, except
he interpret". Paul had it in mind that the speaker in tongues is
also the speaker of its interpretation because the same indwelling spirit gives the vocal ability of tongues and the ability to
reveal its meaning.

There would be no need for Paul to tell the speaker in tongues
to interpret the tongues if the audience could interpret by listening. It is the love-responsibility of the speaker in tongues to see
to it that the audience is given the interpretation. The interpretation is not in the audience. It is in the speaker in tongues to be
spoken out after speaking in tongues.

This means that after listening to a message in tongues, all that
the saints in the audience would have is the tongues they have
heard. The speaker in tongues must not assume that by some
miracle or mysterious means, the audience has the interpretation of what they have heard spoken by another in tongues.

Paul's implied meaning is that ordinarily, the interpretation of
tongues is not with the audience that has listened to the tongues.
It would be usually given by the speaker in tongues. That is obvious since, in his opening statements, Paul gave the divine order
that the person saying something to the church in tongues, must

do so knowing that he or she has spoken in tongues to speak prophecy to that audience.

Paul's teaching is that the target is "that the church may receive edifying". Although the church can hear tongues, since the speaker knows that the interpretation is not with the audience who have listened to tongues, the love-motivation of the speaker in tongues is to give interpretation to the saints who have heard tongues so they can receive edification.

Although the church has heard tongues, their minds cannot receive tongues simply because tongues is not directed at the minds of men. Therefore, the mind of the audience does not understand tongues.

Since the aim is for the church to receive edification and not tongues, the saint who addresses the saints in tongues must understand that his or her gift to the assembled saints is not tongues. He knows that tongues is not the destination but the starting point to arrive at the destination of giving edification by adding something to the tongues.

The mindset encouraged by Paul is that the speaker in tongues must see that he or she is a minister of edification who is using tongues as a vehicle to transfer edification to the minds of the hearers when he or she gives the interpretation of tongues to the audience.

Interpretation of tongues is the bridge between tongues and edification.

Interpretation of tongues is the revelation of tongues to the minds of men who had listened to tongues, so they can be edified. While interpretation is supernatural to the speaker in tongue, it will appear natural to the minds of the audience who are hearing words in the language of their natural minds.

Interpretation of tongues is the giving to the natural minds of men the understanding of what they have heard said in tongues.

Observe that Paul talked about tongues in two different ways in this verse:

First, he spoke about speaking with tongues so that you may prophesy. Afterwards, in his expression, "he that speaketh with tongues, except he interprets", he showed that some were in the habit of speaking in tongues to address the church without progressing to interpretation. This practice of tongues without interpretation was at best a promise to minister to the saints, but the ministry never happened because the speaker in tongues withheld understanding from the assembly, who were not edified as a result.

So Paul showed that the intent of speaking in tongues is that it leads up to what he called "that the church may receive edifying". What causes tongues to not be edifying is not whether it was "genuine" or "fake". In the assembly, if tongues is not properly administered by being interpreted, edification is impossible.

So what did Paul mean by "greater is he that prophesieth"?

This is the text in the AMPLIFIED version:

> Now I wish that all of you spoke in unknown tongues, but even more [I wish] that you would prophesy. The one who prophesies is greater [and more useful] than the one who speaks in tongues, unless he translates or explains [what he says], so that the church may be edified [instructed, improved, strengthened].
> 1 Corinthians 14:5 (AMPLIFIED)

The Amplified version shows that the greater is in usefulness to the church so they can be instructed, improved, strengthened.

This is the same text in the CEV:

I am glad for you to speak unknown languages, although I had rather for you to prophesy. In fact, prophesying does much more good than speaking unknown languages, unless someone can help the church by explaining what you mean.
1 Corinthians 14:5 (CEV)

The CEV brings out the fact that "greater" refers to that which does much more good by helping the church get the explanation or meaning of what has been said.

This is the same text in the Phillips translation:

I should indeed like you all to speak with "tongues", but I would much rather that you all preached the word of God. For the preacher of the word does a greater work than the speaker with "tongues", unless of course the latter interprets his word for the benefit of the Church.
1 Corinthians 14:5 (PHILLIPS)

Likewise, J.B. Phillips shows that greater is better seen as greater work that brings benefit to the church.

This is the same text in The Passion Translation:

I would be delighted if you all spoke in tongues, but I desire even more that you impart prophetic revelation to others. Greater gain comes through the one who prophesies than the one who speaks in tongues, unless there is interpretation so that it builds up the entire church.
1 Corinthians 14:5 (TPT)

The Passion translation shows that greater is better seen as greater gain which is the building up or edification of the church.

Considering the various translations and the overall slant of 1 Corinthians 12, 13, and 14, Paul's "greater" is not concerning the persons speaking or the gifts expressed but the value or work done in edifying the church. "Greater" refers to a target met, an aim realized, or an intention fulfilled.

The man who addressed the assembly in tongues should have edification in mind. If he does not interpret it, that end goal of edifying the saints is not met.

That man who begins to address the assembly in tongues should reach the end goal by prophesying, which means to add interpretation to what had been said in tongues. It is the man that prophesied that met the target, realized the aim, or fulfilled the divine intention of the edification of the saints.

That which is to be done is finally done.

Thus, "greater is he that prophesieth than he that speaketh with tongues" means that the man that prophesied has successfully done that which the man that spoke in tongues without interpretation set out to do but wouldn't do.

Did Paul then forbid tongues? Certainly not. On the contrary he said, "Wherefore, brethren, covet to prophesy, and forbid not to speak with tongues" (1 Corinthians 14:39). The problem was not whether they spoke in tongues or not. The people that Paul addressed spoke in tongues but these speakers in tongues did not progress from addressing the audience in tongues unto the "greater" or "target", which was edification by having interpretation accompany the tongues.

Giving and receiving

5. I would that ye all spake with tongues, but rather that ye

prophesied: for greater **IS** he that prophesieth than he that speaketh with tongues, except he interpret, that the church may receive edifying.
1 Corinthians 14:5

The Greek word translated "that" in "that the church may receive edifying" is **hina**, which means "so that". Paul was teaching about the purpose of the utterance. Thus, the goal of utterance is "that the church may receive edifying".

The goal of utterance is "that the church may receive edifying".

The sure measure of the effectiveness, usefulness, or value of utterance is whether the church received edification or not.

Although speaking in tongues is speaking the vocal abilities of the indwelling spirit, the fact is that a man can speak by the power of the spirit of Christ and fail to give edification to the saints. When this happens, such a saint has not done the "greater" (has not done the job of giving the church edification to receive).

Since the church is receiving the edification, someone must have done the giving that caused this receiving. When addressing the church in tongues, the job of giving the church edification to be received by the church is done by the speaker in tongues and it happens when the speaker in tongues adds interpretation to the tongues.

The man that followed tongues with interpretation provides edification through interpretation accepted by the church.

In a sense, since Paul was teaching on love in 1 Corinthians 14, it is understandable why he was also teaching on giving and receiving. Outside of giving and receiving, love is mere fiction.

When "greater" is used concerning tongues, it means that the audience that has listened to tongues can expect something more. The tongues hint at more to come. This "greater" is ful-filled in the interpretation of tongues. When we add interpreta-tion to tongues we get done the job that tongues had hinted was on the way but tongues alone could not deliver to the minds of the hearers of tongues.

How does the saint go about getting the church to receive edi-fication?

First, there is a message in the heart of the saint. The message is for the audience but they do not yet know it.

The saint with the message in his heart uses tongues to pull the message out of his heart. He starts in tongues. Paul's state-ment "I would that ye all spake with tongues, but rather that ye prophesied" shows that the best way to bring forth utterance in the assembly is via speaking in tongues. Once the messenger has spoken in tongues, the message has left the heart of the speaker but it is not yet with the audience. The audience has only heard tongues. At that point, if the messenger only spoke in tongues, he or she would be "as sounding brass or a tinkling cymbal".

At that point where they have only heard tongues, the minds of the audience need something more than tongues for them to receive edification.

Then the believer who has spoken in tongues gives the message to the church via interpretation. At this point the message is no longer in the heart or mouth of the speaker, but now it is in the ear and mind of the audience. As their minds ponder on the words received, edification is birthed in their minds. The man that interpreted has operated as a giver while the saints whose minds captured what was spoken have operated as receivers.

This "greater" in "greater is he that prophesieth" is the love walk, which cares for the saints by seeing to it that the thing spoken in tongues is interpreted for the benefit of the audience who then have something to receive.

Interpretation of tongues is how the riches possessed in tongues are given to be received by the minds of the audience. The love of God in each believer means that any believer can love the saints by speaking in tongues and using the interpretation of tongues to give edification to the minds of the audience.

Charity in the matter of utterance

1. Follow after charity, and desire spiritual **GIFTS**, but rather that ye may prophesy.
1 Corinthians 14:1

So how do you follow charity in the matter of utterance?

In 1 Corinthians 14:5, you follow charity by starting with tongues and doing the "greater" by adding interpretation to your tongues.

What 1 Corinthians 14:5 calls "greater", 1 Corinthians 14:1 calls "rather that ye may prophesy".

Simply combining 1 Corinthians 14:1 and 1 Corinthians 14:5, when you add interpretation to your tongues, you have prophesied.

You could say it this way: when you add interpretation to your tongues, you have walked in love for you have given the minds of the saints something to receive. Interpretation is the charity that accompanies speaking in tongues.

1. Though I speak with the tongues of men and of angels, and have not charity, I am become **AS** sounding brass, or a tinkling cymbal.
1 Corinthians 13:1

Given the backdrop of 1 Corinthians 14:1 and 1 Corinthians 14:5, the expression "have not charity" is not a reference to not having feelings. It means that although I have spoken in tongues as a messenger, I have not done the "greater" in that I have not added interpretation of tongues to my tongues as a practice of brotherly love.

To interpret tongues, recognise that both the tongues and its interpretation are distinct to the family of God and are available to the man that has believed the gospel. The ability to interpret tongues is not other than or in addition to the ability of tongues.

Since a man can speak in tongues without the saints receiving edification, the love of Christ is more evident in the assembly in the interpretation of tongues than it is in giving a message through tongues. The love that triggered the speaking in tongues must be allowed full expression in the interpretation of tongues. Christ is alive by His spirit in His saints through whom He demonstrates His care. The risen Christ loves His people through us as we administer the interpretation of tongues.

Paul is teaching about the love walk in 1 Corinthians 14. He uses tongues and interpretation, which is prophecy, to teach that lesson.

In both 1 Corinthians 14:1 and 1 Corinthians 14:5, prophecy means to love the saints by edifying them with our utterance. 1 Corinthians 14:5 says this process starts with tongues but must not end there. That which started in tongues must be brought to completion by interpretation. This is "follow after charity" as taught in 1 Corinthians 14:1.

The saint that is tempted to stop at "tongues only" needs to remember that love is equipped with the total ability of edification. The saint also needs to recall that the reason for interpretation of tongues is not to show off, or to flex spiritual muscles but to show love for our brethren.

The implication is that utterance does not exist on its own. It exists to showcase the love of God to our brethren. This is Paul's illustration of the love of God.

Paul gave further instruction to the person who has a message to be delivered via tongues.

The "how-to" of the remedy is given here:

> 5. I would that ye all spake with tongues, but rather that ye prophesied: for greater **IS** he that prophesieth than he that speaketh with tongues, except he interpret, that the church may receive edifying.
> 1 Corinthians 14:5

This should be read with 1 Corinthians 13:1 as the background:

> 1. Though I speak with the tongues of men and of angels, and have not charity, I am become **AS** sounding brass, or a tinkling cymbal.
> 1 Corinthians 13:1

1 Corinthians 14:5's terminology "that the church may receive edifying" shows us the purpose or aim of utterance to bring edification to the assembly.

The saint who had been speaking as an angel or messenger of God in 1 Corinthians 13:1 but had not done the job of edification is now consumed with how the church may receive edifying.

In Paul's solution, which he taught in 1 Corinthians 14:5, he told this person "except he interpret", the church may not receive edifying.

This means that "have not charity" of 1 Corinthians 13:1 is the "except he interpret" of 1 Corinthians 14:5.

In other words, although the church has looked towards the speaker in tongues as an angel (or messenger), the church does not get the message by hearing the tongues. The church cannot receive edification because there has been no interpretation of tongues.

The angel or speaker in tongues will see to it that the audience does not just hear tongues but that the tongues is accompanied by its interpretation. Interpretation of tongues is how the speaker in tongues of angels (one speaking tongues in a non-devotional way) serves the people the edification contained in the message they initially heard as tongues.

Paul distinguished between two modes in which the saints can administer tongues when speaking in tongues of angels (speaking as one with a message for the church).

On the one hand, we have those who speak in tongues of angels but stop at tongues. It is such speakers in tongues, who had a message for the saints but stopped at tongues that Paul had identified as "I speak with the tongues of men and of angels, and have not charity" (see 1 Corinthians 13:1).

On the other hand, and more importantly, there are those speakers in tongues who know that except they interpret, they hinder the church from receiving edification by withholding interpretation of tongues.

When addressing the assembly or speaking in tongues of angels, the edification contained in tongues does not happen by itself. Edification in utterance is not automatic. It is as we "follow after" charity or minister tongues with the understanding that the hearers of tongues have to additionally be interpretation, that the edification takes place. Edification does not jump out of the skies; it must be administered by the speaker in tongues.

The doctrinally sound speaker in tongues knows that the church does not get edified by tongues because tongues is not the end in itself. Starting such messages in tongues tells the assembly to expect more – the interpretation which gives the meaning of the tongues to its hearers so that there might be edification.

> 5. I would that ye all spake with tongues, but rather that ye prophesied: for greater **IS** he that prophesieth than he that speaketh with tongues, except he interpret, that the church may receive edifying.
> 1 Corinthians 14:5

The speaker in tongues, who had a message for the saints starts in tongues knowing that the target is "that the church may receive edifying". It is a scriptural journey from tongues until the destination which is edification. The speaker in tongues of angels adds interpretation as the service of love so that the tongues are understood.

10

THOU VERILY GIVETH THANKS WELL

16. Else when thou shalt bless with the spirit, how shall he that occupieth the room of the unlearned say Amen at thy giving of thanks, seeing he understandeth not what thou sayest? 17. For thou verily givest thanks well, but the other is not edified.
1 Corinthians 14:16-17

Paul had said "he that speaketh in an unknown tongue speaketh not unto men, but unto God" (1 Corinthians 14:2), the primary use of tongues is God-ward, for devotion. Speaking in tongues is a communion between the Father and His family.

He also showed that "if I pray in an unknown tongue, my spirit prayeth" (see 1 Corinthians 14:14). Prayer is God-ward, therefore, tongues is primarily devotional. This is key.

20. But ye, beloved, building up yourselves on your most holy faith, praying in the Holy Ghost,
Jude 1:20

By linking tongues to prayer, Jude emphasized the primary use of tongues in devotion to God. This praying in the Holy Ghost builds up the speaker.

The Greek word translated "building up" in "building up yourselves" is **epoikodomeo**, which means to build upon. It is the combination of **epi** and **oikodomeo**, which is the word that is often translated as edification.

This shows that the speaker in tongues is not built up because of a particular prayer point. The very act and art of communing with the Father by praying in tongues is edification.

> 4. He that speaketh in an **UNKNOWN** tongue edifieth
> himself; but he that prophesieth edifieth the church.
> 1 Corinthians 14:4

The edification spoken of in "He that speaketh in an unknown tongue edifieth himself" is the edifying power of communion with God in the private life. This is the background for 1 Corinthians 14:16-19.

What does it mean to bless with the spirit?

> 16. Else when thou shalt bless with the spirit, how shall he that
> occupieth the room of the unlearned say Amen at thy giving
> of thanks, seeing he understandeth not what thou sayest? 17.
> For thou verily givest thanks well, but the other is not edified.
> 1 Corinthians 14:16-19

To understand Paul's meaning in "bless with the spirit", we recall what he had said in 1 Corinthians 14:14:

> 14. For if I pray in an **UNKNOWN** tongue, my spirit prayeth,
> but my understanding is unfruitful.
> 1 Corinthians 14:14

Paul said, "I pray in an unknown tongue", then he explained praying in tongues as "my spirit prayeth". He was talking about praying in tongues in both instances using different terms. Praying "with my spirit" means to pray in tongues.

Paul appears to have used the term "my spirit" to refer to the tongues that the spirit gives. In the light of his teaching in 1 Corinthians 14:14, "bless with the spirit" in 1 Corinthians 14:16 means to bless with tongues.

Furthermore, Paul described this "bless with the spirit" (in v16) as "thy giving of thanks" (in v17). Therefore, blessing with the spirit is giving thanks in tongues.

The speaker in tongues is giving thanks to God very well (v17). This is communion between God and His saint. This saint giving thanks in tongues is not giving thanks to the brethren.

> **The aim of understanding what was being said in tongues was to encourage the audience to also join in giving thanks in tongues.**

The words spoken while blessing with the spirit, are words not understood by the audience since Paul had explained that "he that speaketh in an unknown tongue speaketh not unto men, but unto God" (1 Corinthians 14:2). Tongues was primarily designed by God with communion in mind. Hence, in 1 Corinthians 14:2 the expression "no man understandeth him" had been used to describe speaking in tongues.

The setting of 1 Corinthians 14:16 is not the private life. The speaker who is blessing with the spirit or giving thanks in tongues is operating like "let him keep silence in the church; and let him speak to himself, and to God" (see 1 Corinthians 14:28).

However, this is not the case of a man speaking to himself and God since he is talking in a way that the others can hear him but those hearing "understandeth not what thou sayest". This fellow could have blessed with the spirit, by speaking privately to himself and God.

In this case, though the man is in the church, he is speaking in tongues but not for the church to hear. His audience is not the church. Although there are other people around, such a man who is "silent in the church", which means with respect to himself he is speaking whereas with regards to the church he is without voice. If he had been in private devotion, he should talk in such a way that it is obvious to the church that he is not addressing them at all. Under such circumstances, the other saints are not his audience. Therefore, no one requires an interpretation. It is perfect praise and the man who has blessed with the spirit is edified.

However, by not speaking to himself and God, in that he is not silent in the church, others can hear him. This was the scenario of the man in 1 Corinthians 14:16. He was in church where others could hear him speaking as one whom the church should listen to. They were listening.

While the man gave thanks, he was talking to God. Since others could hear him, because he spoke as one whom the church should listen to and they listened, he ought to have walked in love towards the onlooking saints.

Therefore, in 1 Corinthians 14:16, the challenge was that the speaker did not speak in a language known to the minds of the hearers but in tongues, and so was not intelligible to the minds of the audience.

To "bless with the spirit" is speaking in a language that the minds of the audience do not understand. Thus, the audience is described as "he that occupieth the room of the unlearned" (v16).

Observe that in 1 Corinthians 14:17, although the mind of the audience did not understand "what thou sayest", the man giving thanks in tongues "verily givest thanks well"!

The other should be edified

> 17. For thou verily givest thanks well, but the other is not edified.
>
> 1 Corinthians 14:17

The speaker praising God in tongues is edified whether the audience says amen to the giving of thanks or not.

What is missing? Although the speaker has given thanks to God well, Paul stated the problem as "the other is not edified". This means that the onlooking church has not been served with the understanding of what it has heard the speaker in tongues say to God in tongues. This "other" refers to those in the audience that are not edified because they do not understand what the speaker in tongues has said.

Men find it impossible to receive edification when they have not received the understanding of words. Since tongues is not a naturally learned vocal ability, its meaning is also not learned. This supernatural understanding of what has been said in tongues comes via the interpretation of tongues. Interpretation of tongues is supernatural to the speaker in tongues but not supernatural to the audience who receive the words in a known language to their minds. Therefore, the audience will treat the meaning conveyed via the interpretation of tongues as they would any other kind of religious communication.

not edified" (v17) after the speaker in tongues had communed with God in thanksgiving very well, he meant that unless interpreted, even tongues spoken in devotion to God does not edify the other brethren in the assembly.

When the speaker in tongues withholds the interpretation of tongues from the audience, the speaker in tongues is not practicing giving and receiving nor following after charity. Paul would say such a speaker in tongues is puffed up. This is the problem of 1 Corinthians 13:1 all over again.

Paul was not condemning but giving corrections. To give correction, we identify that which is not correct and then provide clarity on the answer. If he were condemning, he would have pointed out the wrong and end it there.

The key question was "how shall he that occupieth the room of the unlearned say Amen at thy giving of thanks, seeing he understandeth not what thou sayest?"

We do not say that it does not matter whether the audience is edified or not because what the speaker in tongues is doing is blessing with the spirit.

Paul's question implies that the saints, as an assembly, can worship God at the congregational level in other tongues. The verdict of "thou verily givest thanks well" is a deeply significant statement for it shows that whether the speaker in tongues knows it or not when we speak in tongues we would often be giving thanks well to God.

Tongues is so wonderfully designed for thanksgiving that even when the speaker has not edified the assembly, the divine verdict is still "thou verily givest thanks well".

The fact that blessing with the spirit is giving thanks well is the strongest reason to speak in tongues often.

The speaker in tongues is primarily giving thanks to God. It is not men speaking well of other men. This is directed at God and God considers it effective for thanksgiving even when the speaker has not edified the other saints.

What was Paul's correction?

> 18. I thank my God, I speak with tongues more than ye all:
> 19. Yet in the church I had rather speak five words with my understanding, that **BY MY VOICE** I might teach others also, than ten thousand words in an **UNKNOWN** tongue.
>
> 1 Corinthians 14:18-19

When Paul said, "I speak with tongues more than ye all", he was contrasting between "I speak with tongues" and "you all speak with tongues". He also meant that he spoke tongues in thanksgiving like others, but went even further ("more than") by making the people hear his thanksgiving to God in a language that they understood. This is what he meant by "that by my voice I might teach others also".

His practice "in the church" was "I had rather speak five words with my understanding". The word "rather" there is best translated "most especially". He was emphatic about speaking words with his understanding so others can be taught from what he had spoken to God as thanksgiving.

When he says, "I thank my God", he means that he was thanking God just like the Corinthians who had verily given thanks well in verses 16-17; while "Ye all" referred to the Corinthians who had been giving thanks in tongues well without pursuing the edification of the audience.

Paul was contrasting his thanking God with that of the Corinthians. Certainly, he was not claiming that his thanksgiving in tongues was better than that of another believer. There is no such thing.

The key difference is that he used his thanksgiving to teach whereas the Corinthians had not. He was not teaching God. He interpreted the communion of thanksgiving that he had spoken to God for the benefit of his audience so that it will no longer

be said "thou verily givest thanks well, but the other is not edified" (v17). Unlike the Corinthians who spoke "ten thousand
words in an unknown tongue", Paul spoke his ten thousand
words in an unknown tongue when he was alone. When he is
able to edify the saints, he practiced edification ("in the church I
had rather speak five words with my understanding, that by my
voice I might teach others also").

Thus, "in the church", the Corinthians had given themselves to
speaking thanksgiving in "ten thousand words in an unknown
tongue" and the audience was finding it impossible to receive
edification because there was an abundance of tongues (ten
thousand words in an unknown tongue) but no understanding
of those words.

Paul's "I speak in tongues more than ye all" is not the volume
of tongues spoken in the hearing of the saints but the volume
of edification. It means that the man that gave thanks to God
in tongues very well and also edified the saints has successfully
done that which the man that gave thanks to God in tongues
very well without interpretation set out to do but wouldn't do. It
was a restatement of 1 Corinthians 14:5

> 5. I would that ye all spake with tongues, but rather that ye
> prophesied: for greater **IS** he that prophesieth than he that
> speaketh with tongues, except he interpret, that the church
> may receive edifying.
> 1 Corinthians 14:5

We have already shown that "greater" means that the saints
were edified. The one who prophesied did what ought to have
been done, which the man that spoke in tongues without interpretation omitted. This means that the "greater than" in 1
Corinthians 14:5 and "more than ye all" of 1 Corinthians 14:18
are the same thing – seeing to the edification of the saints.

Observe that the "greater" than the tongues was to let the interpretation of tongues accompany the speaking in tongues so that "the church may receive edifying".

This "more than ye all" was explained as "I had rather speak five words with my understanding". Thus, "I speak with tongues more than ye all" is speaking to men in tongues and then speaking to them in their understanding. This "more than ye all" is administering interpretation to tongues so that the understanding of the audience is enriched.

Paul thanked God in tongues but followed it up with the interpretation of tongues which teaches men in a language that their minds understand.

Thus, in practical terms, and in the context in which Paul has written, Paul's "I speak with tongues more than ye all" is his correction of the Corinthians who were praising God in the presence of the assembly in a way that prevented the congregation from joining in the worship of God.

His rebuke was "how shall he that occupieth the room of the unlearned say Amen at thy giving of thanks".

When the audience can say "Amen at thy giving of thanks", those who said "Amen" have been edified in that they have either joined in praising God in tongues or they have received understanding of those things spoken in praise to God.

Since the emphasis of 1 Corinthians 14 is bringing the assembly into edification by interpreting tongues in the local assembly, the heart of service on the part of the speaker in tongues means the speaker is to watch out for others in the audience saying "Amen at thy giving of thanks".

The aim of understanding what was being said in tongues was to encourage the audience to also join in giving thanks in tongues. Paul said to prioritise the audience getting the interpretation, not leaving the audience to seek the interpretation. Instead, the speaker must supply the interpretation to the audience. Since in the 1 Corinthians 14:16 scenario, the speaker in tongues was thanking God, the solution would be for the audience to receive the understanding of the words spoken in thanksgiving to God. This way, the saints would receive understanding via interpretation and would give thanks together with the original speaker in tongues.

Speak words that teach others

18. I thank my God, I speak with tongues more than ye all:
19. Yet in the church I had rather speak five words with my understanding, that **BY MY VOICE** I might teach others also, than ten thousand words in an **UNKNOWN** tongue.
1 Corinthians 14:18-19

The Greek word translated "yet" in "Yet in the church I had rather speak", is a word that could mean an objection, exception, or a transition to the cardinal matter at hand.

Paul's cardinal concern in 1 Corinthians 14 was stated positively as:

"Let all things be done unto edifying" (see 1 Corinthians 14:26)

"Seek that ye may excel to the edifying of the church" (see 1 Corinthians 14:12)

"That the church may receive edifying" (see 1 Corinthians 14:5)

"Let all things be done decently and in order" (see 1 Corinthians 14:40).

The same cardinal matter is stated negatively as:
"The other is not edified" (see 1 Corinthians 14:17)

Thus, "I speak with tongues more than ye all" is to be read against the background of all things being done unto edification. Although Paul might have spoken in tongues a lot, his point was not by how much his volume of words in tongues exceeded theirs.

He was rather arguing a case for the proper protocol of edification "in the church".

In Corinth, the challenge of edification was not who could out-talk the whole assembly. The challenge was whether the speaker in tongues gave the church understanding or not. Paul was not saying, "add all your tongues together, they are not up to mine". Neither was he implying "you do ten thousand words in tongues while I do one million". He was demonstrating that while they focused on addressing the saints exclusively in tongues, he did more than speak in tongues in that he followed his tongues with interpretation so that "by my voice I might teach others also". If he was teaching them, their minds would have been grasping facts that might otherwise have been unspoken.

18. I thank my God, I speak with tongues more than ye all:
19. Yet in the church I had rather speak five words with my understanding, that **BY MY VOICE** I might teach others also, than ten thousand words in an **UNKNOWN** tongue.
1 Corinthians 14:18-19

Paul does more than tongues. He is additionally speaking words with his understanding. Words spoken in the understanding are addressed to the minds of the audience. Men cannot say they have been taught after hearing words spoken in tongues. He is teaching others by the words which are not spoken in tongues.

Note again that Paul did not compare those who spoke in tongues with others who spoke in understanding. Instead, he has presented two sets of speakers in tongues. In the church, one speaker went on and on in tongues or what Paul described as "ten thousand words in an unknown tongue" while the other interpreted the tongues he spoke himself for the edification of the congregation.

It is this 1 Corinthians 14:19 speaker in "ten thousand words in an unknown tongue" that Paul had described in 1 Corinthians 13:1 as "sounding brass, or a tinkling cymbal". Such a practice is a show-off that is showcasing fluency in tongues. Paul wants such a speaker to pause and switch to speaking in understanding. The word "teach" in "that by my voice I might teach" means to inform orally. The expression "by my voice" is in italics, so it isn't there.

In 1 Corinthians 14:16, the practice of the Corinthians had been to leave the audience not understanding what had been spoken. Where the message of the messenger is unknown to the mind of the audience, the mind is confused, and the church cannot receive edification. Such "messengers" have only blessed with the spirit.

Paul's remedy is that the speaker in tongues, who is giving thanks to God in tongues gives understanding where there had only been tongues previously.

> 19. Yet in the church I had rather speak five words with my understanding, that **BY MY VOICE** I might teach others also, than ten thousand words in an **UNKNOWN** tongue.
> 1 Corinthians 14:19

This verse implies that it is acceptable when not "in the church" but away from the church in the personal space or when in the assembly but not operating as a messenger to the church to speak "ten thousand words in an unknown tongue" without interpretation.

The lesson to be learned in the expression "in the church I had rather speak five words with my understanding" is that the man that can address the church in tongues can also rather or "more especially" speak the understanding of what had been spoken in tongues. Speaking the understanding of what had been spoken in tongues is not a specially granted ability apart from the ability to speak in tongues in the devotional sense in the first place. It is up to the speaker whether to stop at tongues only or to proceed unto giving the understanding of the tongues to the congregation.

The crowd heard two things

4. And they were all filled with the Holy Ghost, and began to speak with other tongues, as the Spirit gave them utterance.

Acts 2:4

At Pentecost, the disciples spoke in what was described as "other" tongues. The Greek word is **heteros**, which is the exact word the Septuagint says Isaiah had used to describe tongues in "stammering lips and another tongue" in Isaiah 28:11. This word **heteros** means another that is not of the same class or kind. This corresponds to Paul's kinds of tongues (1 Corinthians 12:10), which is the language of God's particular family, nation, or tribe that distinguishes it from all others. This is what Jesus had referred to as new tongues, which is a sign that the speaker is of that nation who rest in Zion (from Isaiah 28:16). Note again that "other tongues", indicates that it is a language other than that which men speak by natural ability or by natural training or coaching. It is not a human language. It is lingual abilities from the new birth. It is the vocal abilities of the new creation man. It takes the supernatural ability of the spirit called interpretation of tongues to make sense of what has been spoken in tongues. Even if tongues sound similar to human language, it is not the language of men nor is it languages taught by men.

Since those in the crowd were not saints, they could neither speak in tongues nor could they understand it.

The saints had gathered to pray.

Ordinarily, since tongues is devotional, and the saints had gathered to pray, the speaker in tongues is addressing God (see 1 Corinthians 14:2).

> 6. Now when this was noised abroad, the multitude came together, and were confounded, because that every man heard them speak in his own language.
> Acts 2:6

Since every man in that crowd heard them speak in his language, it means that at some point the crowd understood.

> 11. Cretes and Arabians, we do hear them speak in our tongues the wonderful works of God.
> Acts 2:11

What they heard was "the wonderful works of God". This means that the saints had been praising God similar to 1 Corinthians 14:16. They had been giving thanks very well.

> 16. Else when thou shalt bless with the spirit, how shall he that occupieth the room of the unlearned say Amen at thy giving of thanks, seeing he understandeth not what thou sayest? 17. For thou verily givest thanks well, but the other is not edified.
> 1 Corinthians 14:16-17

On the day of Pentecost, the crowd would have been "he that occupieth the room of the unlearned". According to Paul, they would not what the saints are saying in praise to God. Luke shows that Peter explained that the saints had prophesied (See Acts 2:17-18).

> 5. I would that ye all spake with tongues, but rather that ye prophesied: for greater **IS** he that prophesieth than he that

> speaketh with tongues, except he interpret, that the church
> may receive edifying.
> 1 Corinthians 14:5

Paul explained that prophecy is linked to tongues in that it starts with tongues and is completed by interpretation of tongues.

Therefore, from Luke's record of Peter's explanation in Acts 2:17-18, the reason why the crowd heard "the wonderful works of God" is because the speakers in tongues had additionally exercised the supernatural ability of the spirit called interpretation of tongues to give others the sense of what the saints have been speaking in tongues.

Observe the sequence again:

i.   In Acts 2:4 the saints spoke in other tongues that the crowd did not understand.

ii. In Acts 2:13 "others mocking said, These men are full of new wine" – This fulfilled a prophecy in Psalm 35:16. The crowd that had gathered at the feast of Pentecost were mocking Jesus by mocking that which He had given by His spirit to His saints.

iii. In Acts 2:15, Peter confirmed "these are not drunken, as ye suppose,"

iv. So, the reaction of the crowd to tongues was to mock the speakers in tongues and to conclude that they were drunkards because the crowd did not understand what their fellow countrymen were saying. Then, by prophecy (interpretation of tongues), the crowd heard "the wonderful works of God".

v.   This means the crowd heard two things. First, they heard the praise of God in tongues but they did not know it was the praise of God. They mocked this. They did not understand at this stage. Then, the speakers gave the meaning of the things spoken via interpretation of tongues and the crowd received it. This is what they called the wonderful works of God.

vi. Put differently, per 1 Corinthians 14:16-19, the saints, who were the speakers in tongues used it in communal worship of God, which the crowd mocked because they did not understand. The speakers in tongues were edified and had given thanks well to God but the crowd was not edified. Then the speakers in tongues interpreted it in that they gave the understanding of what they had said in praise.

11

PROPHESYING IN PART

2. And though I have **THE GIFT OF** prophecy, and
understand all mysteries, and all knowledge; and though I
have all faith, so that I could remove mountains, and have not
charity, I am nothing.
1 Corinthians 13:2

The word translated "have" in "I have the gift of
prophecy" means to be closely joined to a person or
a thing or to hold in the hand. It is a possession. The
phrase "the gift of" is in italics. It was added by the translators
so it was not part of the original Greek text. The sentence
should read "And though I have or possess prophecy".

The saint has or possesses prophecy, but this saint was said to
"have not charity".

Prophecy and its purpose

Paul described prophecy and its purpose:
31. For ye may all prophesy one by one, that all may learn, and
all may be comforted.
1 Corinthians 14:31

The Greek word translated "that" is **hina**, which is better translated as "so that" or "so that".

The NIV brings this out better:

> For you can all prophesy in turn so that everyone may be instructed and encouraged.
>
> 1 Corinthians 14:31 (NIV)

> *Charity is our service of ministering edification to others.*

Paul was teaching about the purpose of prophecy. We prophesy so that "all may learn, and all may be comforted". All may be comforted means "all may be edified". The full picture, target, goal, or destination is speaking edification to men. Prophecy is speaking to the assembly for all to be edified (see 1 Corinthians 14:3).

In 1 Corinthians 12, 13, and 14, prophecy was Paul's shorthand for speaking in the assembly to edify the other saints. When addressing the assembly, the saint is not to see speaking in tongues as an end but the door into edifying the saints. If a prophecy is lacking in edification, it is incomplete. It is not whole.

Paul further illustrated prophecy lacking edification:

> 2. And though I have **THE GIFT OF** prophecy, and understand all mysteries, and all knowledge; and though I have all faith, so that I could remove mountains, and have not charity, I am nothing.
>
> 1 Corinthians 13:2

Remember the word translated "charity" means "love".

Recall what Paul had said about charity, which is love:

13. For, brethren, ye have been called unto liberty; only **USE**

not liberty for an occasion to the flesh, but by love serve one
another.
Galatians 5:13

Charity (or love) serves another.

From the 1 Corinthians 13:4 text, Paul showed that the opposite
of charity is "puff up". On the other hand, he had told the Corinthians that charity edifies (see 1 Corinthians 8:1).

> 1. Follow after charity, and desire spiritual **GIFTS**, but rather
> that ye may prophesy.
> 1 Corinthians 14:1

Take note of Paul's instruction to the saints – "follow after charity". Since charity is the edification of others, "follow after charity" is another way of saying, "follow after the edification of
others". This means to "make the edification of others your
aim".

Following after charity means to act
in the light of Christ's service, ministering utterance as love's service
to those believers who are our audience. Since prophesying is following
after charity, it is our practice in the
knowledge of the service of Christ
who laid down His life for us. Thus,
utterance is to be our service in the
knowledge of the service of Christ
who laid down His life for us.

> **"**
> *Prophesying in part*
> *is addressing the*
> *saints in tongues*
> *without pursuing*
> *love which would*
> *see to the edification*
> *of the hearers.*
> **"**

Considering that prophecy is to follow charity, which is serving
others with edification, we are to think of utterance as serving
others so that edification might come forth.

Said a little differently, since charity edifies and charity is service, charity is our service of ministering edification to others. Therefore, we could also say that "follow after charity" means to "to serve another with the advantage or edification of that person in mind".

> 2. And though I have **THE GIFT OF** prophecy, and understand all mysteries, and all knowledge; and though I have all faith, so that I could remove mountains, and have not charity, I am nothing.
> 1 Corinthians 13:2

Therefore, to "have not charity" means not to serve others with the edification of that person in mind.

What Paul had described as having prophecy but not having charity is not a thing of praise for he meant that as a violation of the love law by those who do not follow in the footsteps of Christ which serves others.

Paul's point in talking about "have not charity" while discussing prophecy which is the service of edification is that prophecy can be administered wrongly in that it is not administered as a service of edification to the saints.

Just as 1 Corinthians 13:1 is a statement of a problem, "have not charity" in 1 Corinthians 13:2 is also a restatement of the problem identified in 1 Corinthians 13:1 – not supply the service that edifies another.

Paul gave an illustration of prophecy as the practice of love:

> 5. I would that ye all spake with tongues, but rather that ye prophesied: for greater **IS** he that prophesieth than he that speaketh with tongues, except he interpret, that the church may receive edifying.
> 1 Corinthians 14:5

The word translated "rather" in "rather that ye prophesied" means more especially.

The Greek word translated "that" in "that the church may re-ceive edifying" is **hina**, which means "so that". Paul's point was that the purpose or aim of tongues, interpre-tation, and prophecy was that "the church may receive edifying".

> ❝
> *The knowledge that puffs up in 1 Corinthians 8:1 is the knowledge that has the edification component missing.*
> ❞

The purpose or aim of interpreted tongues addressed to the assembly is so that the church can receive edification. Since the church receives edification, to get the job done, the speaker who started in tongues is to give the interpretation to them.

He showed that addressing men via tongues by itself could not edify the church. If we aim to address men and we start with tongues, we must add the interpretation so that "the church may receive edifying" via understanding.

What does it mean to know in part?

9. For we know in part, and we prophesy in part.
1 Corinthians 13:9

The word translated "part" in 1 Corinthians 13:9 means a por-tion, a piece, or that which is one of the constituent parts of a whole. It is not the whole. Something is missing.

The reader must call to mind what Paul had already stated in 1 Corinthians 8 regarding knowledge.

1. Now as touching things offered unto idols, we know that we

all have knowledge. Knowledge puffeth up, but charity edifieth.
1 Corinthians 8:1

There is a knowledge that puffs up and a knowledge that "edifieth".

10 For if any man see thee which hast knowledge sit at meat in the idol's temple, shall not the conscience of him which is weak be emboldened to eat those things which are offered to idols; 11 And through thy knowledge shall the weak brother perish, for whom Christ died? 12 But when ye sin so against the brethren, and wound their weak conscience, ye sin against Christ.
1 Corinthians 8:10-12

The knowledge is not the issue but the use of the knowledge. The man with knowledge can use it to make the weak brother perish. This perishing refers to wounding the conscience by emboldening a man to act out that which his conscience is convinced is wrong. The wounded conscience brings condemnation to the man that has eaten that which his heart forbids. In such cases, the man with knowledge has sinned against the brethren and so sinned against Christ. He has practiced selfishness.

This shows that knowledge by itself is not edification. It is missing the part that edifies. It is the correct use of knowledge that edifies. Knowledge is one key side to the coin of edification but it is not the only side.

If edification is the whole, knowledge is one part, the use of knowledge is the other part. Edification is not just the content of knowledge. It is the use of knowledge that brings or withholds edification.

Paul used the same knowledge differently:

13 Wherefore, if meat make my brother to offend, I will eat

no flesh while the world standeth, lest I make my brother to
offend.
1 Corinthians 8:13

Whereas a knowledgeable saint had abused knowledge to crush
the conscience of the saints, Paul correctly used the same
knowledge to edify the brethren.

The part that Paul added to the knowledge, which was missing in the other who abused knowledge was that he served the
brethren and preferred them in love by choosing not to enforce
the exercise of liberty that he had.

This is the knowledge that edifies another.

This knowledge that edifies another is allowed to have its full
impact in and through the one possessing the knowledge. The
other kind of knowledge puffs up. This shows that knowledge
by itself is not equal to edification. It is how the knowledge is
used that edifies or not.

4. Charity suffereth long, **AND** is kind; charity envieth not;
charity vaunteth not itself, is not puffed up,
1 Corinthians 13:4

"Puff up" is being focused on self or lacking in service. It is the
opposite of kindness or long-suffering (charity). It is lacking in
edification. Thus, when service is not added to knowledge, what
is missing is edification. Such knowledge is in part. That part
that edifies is missing.

Thus, the knowledge that puffs up in 1 Corinthians 8:1 is the
knowledge that has the edification component missing in that it
does not serve the brethren in love.

What does it mean to prophesy in part?

9. For we know in part, and we prophesy in part.

1 Corinthians 13:9

> **The way out of prophesying in part is to grow spiritually by thinking and understanding differently.**

Given that knowledge in part is knowledge lacking in edification, "prophesy in part" would be the prophecy or utterance that puffs up, which is utterance lacking in edification. Thus, prophesy in part is utterance not administered as a service of edification to the saints. The speaker is not abiding by the edification principle.

Prophesy in part is not recognising that utterance, just as with knowledge, utterance by itself does not edify.

Just as in 1 Corinthians 8:1, knowledge can be used in such a way that the edification component is missing, in 1 Corinthians 13:9 prophecy can be used in such a way that the edification component is also missing. Hence Paul's "we know in part, and we prophesy in part".

Whether knowledge or prophecy, when edification, which is serving the saints, is missing, it is referred to as "in part".

We have shown in 1 Corinthians 13:1-2, that to "have not charity" means the speaker in tongues is not serving others with the edification of the audience in mind. From the perspective of the assembly, when tongues is left to itself and not joined to the interpretation of tongues, the tongues is in part or incomplete in that it has failed to edify the church.

Since charity edifies, the tongues spoken "without charity" is not whole in that it cannot edify the saints who have been addressed in tongues. Utterance has been given but it is still lacking in meeting love's standard of the edification of the saints.

Paul's "we prophesy in part" is not praiseworthy, for it means that love's aim of edification is unfulfilled.

Thus, to prophesy in part is to address the saints in tongues without interpretation of tongues, which achieves precisely zero edification.

> 1. Now concerning spiritual **GIFTS**, brethren, I would not
> have you ignorant.
> 1 Corinthians 12:1

When Paul had said, "concerning spiritual gifts, brethren, I would not have you ignorant", it is this ignorance, which is not so much a lack of knowledge but that unpersuadableness towards preferring another in love that he addresses. It was the knowledge of the edification principle that had been ignored.

In 1 Corinthians 13:9, "in part" describes the implications of their being ignorant about the administration of spirituals. Paul illustrated this "we prophesy in part" much later in 1 Corinthians 14:

> 16. Else when thou shalt bless with the spirit, how shall he that
> occupieth the room of the unlearned say Amen at thy giving
> of thanks, seeing he understandeth not what thou sayest? 17.
> For thou verily givest thanks well, but the other is not edified.
> 1 Corinthians 14:16-17

Although the speaker in tongues had given thanks in tongues well, Paul implied that such a saint had not met love's standard of edifying the other saints. We know this because his brethren who are his audience "understandeth not what thou sayest", as a result of which Paul says, "the other is not edified".

He meant that in a public setting, the utterance, which should have been used to pursue the edification of the brethren had been used as private communion between the speaker and God.

Again, Paul gives the purpose of utterance:

> 26. How is it then, brethren? when ye come together, every one of you hath a psalm, hath a doctrine, hath a tongue, hath a revelation, hath an interpretation. Let all things be done unto edifying.
> 1 Corinthians 14:26

The "all things" to be done unto edifying are the giving of the psalm, doctrine, tongues, revelation, and interpretation.

Addressing the saints in tongues and interpretation is to be done unto edifying.

Since utterance is to be administered with edification in mind when the utterance is given but the saints are not edified, the utterance is in part or incomplete, and such uninterpreted tongues is prophesying in part.

> 9. For we know in part, and we prophesy in part.
> 1 Corinthians 13:9

Therefore, what Paul referred to as "in part", he had earlier stated as "have not charity" (see 1 Corinthians 13:1-2), for both expressions mean not having the edification of the saints in mind.

So, the speaker who is addressing the assembly starts out speaking in tongues, which is a valid portion.

That speaker realises that using speaking in tongues to address the assembly is just the beginning and by no means the full portion.

That speaker knows that until interpreted, the full portion, which is edification, is not administered and so the saints are not served.

Prophesying in part is addressing the saints in tongues without pursuing love which would see to the edification of the hearers.

It is because we know in part that we prophesy in part. In other words, a person that ignores the instructions on edification will not use utterance, to edify the audience.

"We know in part" does not mean that as saints we will never know the word of God. It does not mean that some people would know some things and others would know another, while God ensures that none of us know His word. If this was true, we would have to question even what Moses, the prophets, the psalmists, the gospel writers, and the apostles have written, for whatever they have written cannot be complete. Ironically, if we take that way of reasoning seriously, it would mean that the statement "we know in part" is also not complete since Paul who wrote it only knew a fraction of the truth.

> 3. How that by revelation he made known unto me the mystery; (as I wrote afore in few words, 4. Whereby, when ye read, ye may understand my knowledge in the mystery of Christ)
> Ephesians 3:3-4

Paul had supernatural knowledge that he wrote down for the benefit of the readers of his letter to the Ephesians. He was certain that this knowledge becomes theirs as they read. The believer is to have clear, detailed knowledge.

Put away childish things

Did Paul classify himself among the "we" in "we know in part"?

He wrote:

> 11. When I was a child, I spake as a child, I understood as a
> child, I thought as a child: but when I became a man, I put
> away childish things.
> 1 Corinthians 13:11

This "I spake as a child" was another way of stating "I am become as sounding brass, or a tinkling cymbal" (see 1 Corinthians 13:1 – KJV). It was his summary of his administration of utterance. He wanted the Corinthians to know that he had also previously prophesied in part.

By "I put away childish things", he meant that he stopped his practice of prophesying in part. It did not happen magically. It was deliberate. He stopped violating the love law of edification and put "childish things" or prophesying in part away.

He couldn't put childish things away for as long as he understood as a child and thought as a child.

"When I became a man" means Paul let the word change his thinking and understanding and as a result, he no longer practiced prophesying in part.

His correction in 1 Corinthians 12, 13, and 14 was his correction of thinking and understanding as a child.

By implication, prophesying in part is not because the saint lacks the ability or power to complete the task at hand. "Prophesying in part" is bad behaviour from incomplete thinking and incomplete understanding, which fails to see that utterance is to serve edification to the saints. It is incomplete thinking and misunderstanding that causes the child to celebrate addressing the assembly in uninterpreted tongues. The man who has "put away childish things" says "in the church I had rather speak five words with my understanding, that by my voice I might teach

others also, than ten thousand words in an unknown tongue (1
Corinthians 14:19 – KJV)".

17. For thou verily givest thanks well, but the other is not
edified.
1 Corinthians 14:17

The saint who has been identified as the child in 1 Corinthians 13:11 will say, "from 1 Corinthians 14:2, the primary use
of tongues is God-ward, and for devotion. Therefore, when I
praise God in tongues, I build up or edify myself (1 Corinthians
14:4), and that while addressing God I am blessing with the
spirit (1 Corinthians 14:16) and in response to such excellent
praise, God himself says, "thou gives thanks well" (1 Corinthians 14:17), what more could I do since God has already said I
gave thanks well?"

On the other hand, Paul's "man" of 1 Corinthians 13:11 fully
agrees that the primary use of tongues is God-ward, for devotion, for "he that speaketh in an unknown tongue speaketh not
unto men, but unto God" (1 Corinthians 14:2). He agrees that
God prizes thanksgiving in tongues for God himself says, "thou
gives thanks well" (1 Corinthians 14:17). In distinction, this man
puts away the childish thinking that fails to see that in 1 Corinthians 14:16, the setting is not the private life, for the speaker in
tongues is not speaking to himself and God but in the hearing
of the whole assembly. Therefore, the thinking should shift to
giving the saints the service of edification which is required in
the assembly. As a result, rather than adopting the mindset that
causes the child to say, "what more could I do?", the man knows
there is much more to do and proceeds to interpret the things
said to God for the benefit of the minds of the other saints so
that by getting understanding, they get edified.

The child's way of thinking and understanding is prophesying
in part.

In contrast, the man who has "put away childish things" has done the greater in that he has edified the saints.

The man who "had rather speak five words with my understanding, that by my voice I might teach others also, than ten thousand words in an unknown tongue" (1 Corinthians 14:19) has hit the target of edification. The man who addresses "ten thousand words in an unknown tongue" without teaching others also (1 Corinthians 14:19) has prophesied in parts.

The child would say "the only thing I have from God is tongues".

The man who has put away childish things would say instead, "The believer has received more than tongues in the indwelling of the holy ghost. In that indwelling, the believer all that is required for edification. Therefore, because edification demands it, the saint gives forth tongues and follows it up with the interpretation of tongues".

The child has the same ability of tongues that the man has but does not minister it correctly due to incomplete understanding or wrong thinking.

The man who puts away childish things does not have more spirit or ability. He heeds Paul's instructions which enrich his understanding and thought. This results in better administration of the vocal abilities of the spirit.

How else did Paul explain this "I put away childish things"?

> 5. I would that ye all spake with tongues, but rather that ye prophesied: for greater **IS** he that prophesieth than he that speaketh with tongues, except he interpret, that the church may receive edifying.
> 1 Corinthians 14:5

Paul's term "greater" is with respect to the purpose or goal, which is "that the church may receive edifying".

In the assembly, the man that stopped at addressing the assembly in tongues without interpretation has not done the "greater" in that the saints are not edified. It is the man that prophesied that has successfully done that which the man that spoke in tongues without interpretation set out to do but would not do.

When it comes to the assembly, prophecy is speaking so that the church can receive edification.

If it were the private life, the speaker in tongues does not need to prophesy to receive edification.

Thus, from the perspective of the assembled saints, where "receiving edification" is the target or the measurement of the whole, tongues is an incomplete prophecy in that it fails to edify.

To prophesy fully will be to give interpretation to tongues, while prophesying in part will be to speak forth tongues and stop at tongues.

It is faulty thinking which assumes that the speaker only has tongues and that the audience will sort themselves out by obtaining interpretation, which is some additional far-away power to be acquired after receiving yet more power. Since the target, goal, whole, or the full intent of God, in the assembly, is edification, anything short of edification is "in part".

> 9. So likewise ye, except ye utter by the tongue words easy to be understood, how shall it be known what is spoken? for ye shall speak into the air.
> 1 Corinthians 14:9

"Words easy to be understood" refers to giving the full portion, by giving the interpretation, rather than stopping mid-purpose and treating an opportunity to serve the saints as though it was personal between the speaker and God.

While the audience can say, "how shall it be known what is spoken, the speaker in tongues cannot say the same. this is because Paul never taught the speaker in tongues to leave it to the audience to seek the interpretation of what they had heard in tongues.

If the assembly is saying "how shall it be known what is spoken", it is because the speaker in tongues has "spoken into the air", which is the same thing as prophesying in part.

Paul used various terms to explain "prophesying in part" (1 Corinthians 13:9):

I am become as sounding brass, or a tinkling cymbal (1 Corinthians 13:1).

I spake as a child (1 Corinthians 13:11).

Speak into the air (1 Corinthians 14:9).

He that speaketh shall be a barbarian unto me (1 Corinthians 14:11).

… ten thousand words in an unknown tongue (1 Corinthians 14:19).

These terms are the same thing stated differently. They describe what is incomplete about prophesying in part.

Given that Paul said, "but when I became a man, I put away childish things" (see 1 Corinthians 3:11), we conclude that the "we" in 1 Corinthians 13:9 is not every Christian. It accurately describes all those Christians who prophesy in part.

That which is perfect

10. But when that which is perfect is come, then that which is
in part shall be done away.
1 Corinthians 13:10

What does Paul mean by "that which is perfect"?

The expression "that which is perfect" means that which wants nothing to complete it. It means fully grown, mature or full age or to finish. It speaks of completion or getting a job done.

Paul expands this "that which is perfect" in the next verse.

11. When I was a child, I spake as a child, I understood as a
child, I thought as a child: but when I became a man, I put
away childish things.
1 Corinthians 13:11

Rather than say "that which is perfect", he says, "I became a man". The man is the one that puts away childish things.

Recall that "childish things" refers to the speaker who addresses the assembly in tongues and then falling short of edifying the saints because of wrong thinking or understanding which resulted in neglecting the ability already possessed in the indwelling spirit – i.e., neglecting the fact that the ability of tongues and the ability of interpretation is the same.

In other words, the childish thing would be to treat "that which is in part" (see 1 Corinthians 13:10) as though it were the whole.

The whole or complete is "except he interpret, that the church may receive edifying" (see 1 Corinthians 14:5). Interpretation brings understanding to the audience so that they are edified.

11. When I was a child, I spake as a child, I understood as a

> child, I thought as a child: but when I became a man, I put
> away childish things.
> 1 Corinthians 13:11

"I put away childish things" is not the putting away of revelation knowledge or the abandonment of giving utterance in
tongues; it is the putting away of treating "that which is in part"
as though it were the whole, preferring the saints in love and
prioritizing the edification of the saints.

When addressing a message to the church, speaking to them
in tongues only is prophesying in part. When the speaker in
tongues adds interpretation, the "whole" replaces the "part"
and as a result, the saints can receive the interpretation as edification.

Having something to say is a part and not the whole. Ministering what we have so that the saints are edified is the other part
that completes the understanding.

> 10. But when that which is perfect is come, then that which is
> in part shall be done away.
> 1 Corinthians 13:10

Here, Paul meant that "that which is perfect" or mature and
complete replaced that which was in part.

In the Greek text, the expression "shall be done away" is one
Greek word katargeo, which means to make something expire,
to render inactive, put to an end, or separate.

The perfect puts an end to the part.

In other words, from the perspective of the audience, when the
speaker gives a prophecy in full, the interpretation of tongues
gives understanding that separates the audience from lack of
edification.

From the speaker's perspective, putting away childish things by giving prophecy in full as the interpretation of tongues to the audience, so they could be edified, separates the speaker from operating as a child who thinks only of self to one who serves others in love.

As the saint is given to the practice of love, the part disappears. The way out of prophesying in part is to grow spiritually by thinking and understanding differently. Heeding the apostolic instructions, which is spiritual growth, sacks, expires, or puts out of action the selfishness which does not edify. Thus, "that which is perfect" is putting away the childish things by operating as a man that edifies the saints.

In conclusion, Paul's expression "that which is perfect" is not a reference to life after death, some far away dimension of living or life in the sweet by and by. He wasn't discussing any of those things. In context, it is the edification of the saints as a discharge of our stewardship of the abilities given in the spirit of God.

THE SPIRITS OF THE PROPHETS

32. And the spirits of the prophets are subject to the prophets.
1 Corinthians 14:32

Where is the setting for discussing the prophets?

These prophets are in the church.

So what do these prophets do? The prophets speak to the church.

29. Let the prophets speak two or three, and let the other judge.
1 Corinthians 14:29

These prophets, who speak to the church will be the men who are speaking in the tongues of angels or speaking as messengers to the assembly (see 1 Corinthian 13:1).

What are the characteristics of these prophets?

37. If any man think himself to be a prophet, or spiritual, let

him acknowledge that the things that I write unto you are the
commandments of the Lord.

1 Corinthians 14:37

> **The prophet is
> not just one who
> speaks in tongues
> but one who
> distinguishes self
> in edifying the
> saints.**

Paul referred to the prophet as the
spiritual. This speaker that Paul referred to as spiritual is not some
goofy fellow going everywhere telling visions to men and women. A
prophet is not primarily a seer of
visions. The prophet is a minister
of the word. Paul said, let him (the
prophet) acknowledge. The Greek
word translated acknowledge is the
Greek word **epiginosko**, a word
that means a thorough and detailed knowledge of what Paul
had written.

The prophet is not just one who speaks in tongues but one
who distinguishes self in edifying the saints. Given the emphasis
on the right knowledge, the prophet or spiritual ministers from
spiritual growth.

9. And as they came down from the mountain, Jesus charged
them, saying, Tell the vision to no man, until the Son of man
be risen again from the dead.

Matthew 17:9

Jesus' command to Peter, James, and John means that seeing a
vision does not qualify the seer to say anything about it.

Since they were to "tell the vision to no man, until the Son of
man be risen again from the dead", it would be in their knowledge of the resurrection that they would receive understanding. From this understanding they became believers and became
preachers of the message of the gospel. In the light of the resurrection, they would know what to emphasize in retelling the

vision to people.

> **We do not say all that we see – it is not wise.**

This shows that there is more maturity required in the retelling of visions than in seeing the visions in the first place. This is true whether this is a bona fide vision or a fluke. We know that seeing visions is not the big deal because before Cornelius received eternal life, he saw in a vision accurately (see Acts 10:3).

On the mount of transfiguration, before Peter, James and John received eternal life, they saw in a vision accurately. Likewise, after Paul received eternal life, he saw in a vision accurately (see Acts 22:17-21).

Anyone can see a vision – saints and non-saints alike.

The big lesson learned is that as seers of visions, Peter and the other disciples were not to tell that vision until they had a revelation of the resurrection. It is in the truth of the resurrection that we understand where to place our emphasis in retelling visions.

It is one thing to see accurately and another thing to say accurately. Seeing accurately and saying accurately are different thing.

To say accurately requires discipleship. Saying scripturally that which has been seen in a vision requires the student of the word to ponder and diligently study the vision in the light of the written word to be able to use it to edify. In between seeing a vision and saying is a lot of discipleship.

This is so because a vision could be genuine, accurate, and precise but what is ministered through it by the one who has seen the vision does not edify.

Visions and other supernatural experiences are not in themselves edification, only a bona fide way of grabbing the attention of men.

> 45. Then opened he their understanding, that they might understand the scriptures,
> Luke 24:45

After the resurrection of Jesus, He opened the understanding of his disciples so that they saw the scriptures as a testimony of Christ. It was by receiving the resurrection fact that they became believers. They became students of the resurrection and preachers of the same to others. In the light of the resurrection, they then knew what to emphasize in retelling the vision to people.

> *Visions and other supernatural experiences are not in themselves edification, only a bona fide way of grabbing the attention of men.*

Given Jesus' instruction here, the prophet would not be known in his or her ability to see a vision but in the ability to submit the vision to the principle of edification and speak in that light to the saints.

A person has not faithfully served the saints just by seeing an accurate God-given vision. The vision conveys a message. That message must be subjected to the written word and must be told only because it meets the criteria of edification. It must be told in a way that strengthens persuasion in the written word.

After he received the knowledge of the resurrection, John had other God-given visions later in his ministry.

Edification is the Revelation of Jesus Christ

1. The Revelation of Jesus Christ, which God gave unto him,
to shew unto his servants things which must shortly come to
pass; and he sent and signified IT by his angel unto his servant
John: 2. Who bare record of the word of God, and of the
testimony of Jesus Christ, and of all things that he saw.
Revelation 1:1-2

The visions were John's record of the word of God which is the
testimony of Jesus Christ.

3. Blessed **IS** he that readeth, and they that hear the words of
this prophecy, and keep those things which are written therein:
for the time IS at hand.
Revelation 1:3

John wrote the vision down so people could read it. He referred
to his writing of the vision as prophecy. Thus, prophecy can
originate from visions.

Paul gave the rules for prophecy in 1 Corinthians 12, 13, and 14.

The telling of a vision is utterance therefore it is governed by
the rules of edification.

11. Saying, I am Alpha and Omega, the first and the last: and,
What thou seest, write in a book, and send **IT** unto the seven
churches which are in Asia; unto Ephesus, and unto Smyrna,
and unto Pergamos, and unto Thyatira, and unto Sardis, and
unto Philadelphia, and unto Laodicea.
Revelation 1:11

Jesus is the Alpha and Omega. He is the last or the completion
or the finisher of God's plan from the beginning (from Gen-

esis).

Jesus' instruction was "What thou seest, write in a book".

Jesus' instruction for John to write things in a book means that what John wrote in a book is to be in line with the other books of the bible.

Thus, the telling of a vision is governed by the written word.

> 12. And I turned to see the voice that spake with me. And being turned, I saw seven golden candlesticks; 13. And in the midst of the seven candlesticks **ONE** like unto the Son of man, clothed with a garment down to the foot, and girt about the paps with a golden girdle.
> Revelation 1:12-13

Observe that amid John's visions was "one like unto the Son of man". Christ was at the heart of John's visions and he wrote or prophesied from that slant.

Observe the centrality of Christ in John's writing:

I am Alpha and Omega (Revelation 1:11)

The first and the last (Revelation 1:11)

Him which is, and which was, and which is to come (Revelation 1:4)

The Son of man (Revelation 1:12)

The Revelation of Jesus Christ (Revelation 1:1)

If Christ was not at the heart of John's visions, there would be nothing of his visions worth telling to the churches. If John had tried to tell the vision apart from the Revelation of Jesus

Christ, the Lord Jesus would have told him to "tell the vision to no man".

4. John to the seven churches which are in Asia: Grace **BE** unto you, and peace, from him which is, and which was, and which is to come; and from the seven Spirits which are before his throne;

Revelation 1:4

John's visions were for the seven churches in Asia.

Those words "Grace be unto you, and peace" are the same words used to introduce the fulfilment of redemption to the churches in the epistles (see 1 Corinthians 1:3, 2 Cor 1:2, Gal 1:3, Eph 1:2). John's use of these words shows us that John prophesied from

> *The prophets' actions when prophesying are subject to the prophets.*

the truth of redemption. It was as John, Peter, and James developed as students of the grace of God that they could tell their visions.

In telling his vision, John started from the truth of redemption. What he would say would be guided by his knowledge of the accomplishment of Christ in redemption. Thus, for the saint, the (re)telling of a vision is not merely replaying images and saying anything that comes to mind.

7. He that hath an ear, let him hear what the Spirit saith unto the churches; To him that overcometh will I give to eat of the tree of life, which is in the midst of the paradise of God.

Revelation 2:7

Observe that in retelling his vision as prophecy, John did not say, "He that hath an eye, let him see what the Spirit showed me".

He did not tell them his visions so that they too could see the same visions that he had seen. The key was "he that hath an ear, let him hear what the Spirit saith".

John pointed them at what the spirit said – the revelation of Jesus!

> 3. Blessed **IS** he that readeth, and they that hear the words of this prophecy, and keep those things which are written therein: for the time **IS** at hand.
> Revelation 1:3

The Greek word translated "readeth" is **anaginosko**, which relates to comprehensive, repetitive assimilation of facts.

The person who was blessed wouldn't be the person trying to see John's visions, it'll be the person "that readeth" what John wrote after what he had seen in the vision.

There was no edification in John's seeing a vision. There will be no edification in anyone trying to see that vision today. The people were not blessed in seeing the vision all over again.

John's service to the saints was not in seeing the vision but in documenting it to reveal Jesus. In this case, prophecy was in John's understanding of how to say the message contained in the vision so the hearers can receive edification. This means John would not say certain things until he knew how to minister it in a way that edifies. We do not say all that we see – it is not wise.

In John's writing, we see in a clear manner, how to edify the church with a prophecy even if it had originated from a vision.

He was not trying to scare his audience. He gave them a revelation of Jesus (see Revelations 1:1). People were scared before they read John's writings. John's writings exposed the fears that had been lurking in their minds. There is blessedness in reading John's writings as a revelation of redemption.

37. If any man think himself to be a prophet, or spiritual, let him acknowledge that the things that I write unto you are the commandments of the Lord.
1 Corinthians 14:37

Paul's prophet is the spiritual, who acknowledges.

The word translated acknowledge is the Greek word **epiginosko,** a word that means a thorough and detailed knowledge of Paul's writings (and the explanation of the apostles too). The prophet is not just one who speaks in tongues but also has clarity from the apostolic writings and ministers edification to the saints from that clear and detailed understanding of Paul's writings. The prophet does not ignore Paul's instructions concerning utterance.

The spirits of the prophets

32. And the spirits of the prophets are subject to the prophets.
1 Corinthians 14:32

Since we can substitute spiritual for the prophet, we can render this text as "the spirits of the spiritual are subject to them".

We can also state it as "the spirits of those saints who minister from a clear and detailed understanding of Paul's writings are subject to them".

What does Paul mean by "the spirits" in "the spirits of the prophets are subject to the prophets"?

Given that he spoke of prophets, and he had said concerning

the prophets, "let the prophets speak" (1 Corinthians 14:29 – KJV), the things that are subject to the prophets (the spiritual or saints given to a comprehensive understanding of the spirit by the gospel) are those things that these prophets say in the congregation.

Therefore, rather than say, "the spirits of the prophets are subject to the prophets", we can say "the sayings or utterance spoken by the prophets are subject to the prophets."

In the verse before "the spirit of the prophet is subject to the prophet", Paul had said, "ye may all prophesy one by one, that all may learn, and all may be comforted" (see 1 Corinthians 14:31). His immediate context for "spirits" was prophecy or interpreted tongues in the assembly.

Therefore, rather than say, "the spirits of the prophets are subject to the prophets", we can also say:

"The prophesyings or utterances that bring clarity through the prophets are subject to the prophets"

More clearly, the point made is that "the prophets' actions when prophesying are subject to the prophets".

> 3. But he that prophesieth speaketh unto men **TO** edification, and exhortation, and comfort.
> 1 Corinthians 14:3

All that the prophet speaks to the congregation are spoken unto their edification.

> 26. How is it then, brethren? when ye come together, every one of you hath a psalm, hath a doctrine, hath a tongue, hath a revelation, hath an interpretation. Let all things be done unto edifying.
> 1 Corinthians 14:26

All that the prophet speaks to the congregation are regulated by the wider concept of "let all things be done unto edifying".

Paul's "the spirits of the prophets are subject to the prophets" is not another topic but the lesson that the prophets' actions when prophesying are subject to the prophets' heeding what the apostles have taught regarding the edification principle".

Thus, what Paul meant by the expression "the spirits of the prophets are subject to the prophets" is that it is up to the spiritual or knowledgeable saints, to let their knowledge of the word subject them to the principle of edification.

It is obvious that the prophets' actions when prophesying are subject to the prophets when we observe the following:

> 31. For ye may all prophesy one by one, that all may learn, and all may be comforted.
> 1 Corinthians 14:31

Given that prophecy is tongues and interpretation of tongues, rather than say, "ye may all prophesy one by one", we can say, "ye may all speak in tongues followed by interpretation one by one".

Paul's lesson in "the spirits of the prophets are subject to the prophets" was that there is order. He later referred to this as "let all things be done decently and in order" (1 Corinthians 14:40 – KJV).

"The spirit of the prophets are subject to the prophets" means that all that speak in utterance are not to do so as though controlled by some invisible external power moving their mouths against their wills.

"The spirits" in "the spirits of the prophets are subject to the prophets" would be referring to the things said as prophecy or as tongues and interpretation of tongues.

We observe that before his statement "the spirits of the prophets are subject to the prophets", Paul had taught:

> 28. But if there be no interpreter, let him keep silence in the church; and let him speak to himself, and to God.
> 1 Corinthians 14:28

If there be no interpreter means if the one speaking will not obey the rules of edification. Paul's point was that if the one who is to address the church is not doing so to interpret, he is to keep silent in the church rather than address the whole church.

Even under inspiration, the prophets, the spiritual or knowledgeable saints, are not overpowered by some unexplainable force to say the things that they speak out as prophecy or as tongues and interpretation of tongues

"The spirits of the prophets are subject to the prophets" describes the practice of self-control evident in those who are knowledgeable about spiritual things. The things of the spirit are under the stewardship of the saint, who is responsible for conducting himself in ways to maximise edification.

They know when to be silent in the church and when to speak.

They know they are ministers who are subject to those instructions that the apostles have given concerning the edification principle.

They also know that might mean slowing down to give the interpretation of the tongues or even repeating the interpretation of a tongue that they had already given because the principle of edification demands it so that the audience can flow along.

Thus, "the spirits" in "the spirits of the prophets are subject to the prophets" does not refer to the indwelling spirit as God's gift in redemption. We are never commanded to subject the indwelling spirit of God to anything. Instead, by the written word, we subject our thoughts and practice to the indwelling spirit.

For clarity, "the spirits" is a figure of speech referring to the tongues spoken, the interpretation that should follow the tongues, and the various other things we say by inspiration to the brethren.

Although the KJV says "the spirits", the term in Greek is just "spirit". Since the term "the spirits" refers to the prophecy, tongues, interpretation, and the various other things we say by the inspiration of the indwelling spirit, a clearer way of rephrasing the verse would be "and spirits spoken by prophets are subject to prophets". There are no definite articles in that verse at all in the Greek text. It is clearer that the spirit refers to the various utterances. It is also clearer that Paul did not have specific prophets in mind when he wrote as he did. It was a general instruction for the whole assembly.

Scholars say that the expression "the spirits" is the figure of speech - metonymy. For example, business executives wear suits. If instead of business executive, I say "suit", I have used suit as metonymy in place of a business executive. If I say the car belongs to the crown, I have used crown to refer to the Queen of England. In this case, in Paul's letter, the indwelling spirit gives us things to say. This is a part of what the spirit gives. It is a characteristic of the spirit. The spirit is also the ability to see, know and perceive. There is more to the indwelling spirit than utterance. If I use "spirit" to refer to an utterance that is a characteristic of indwelling spirit, I have used "spirit" as a metonymy.

In other words, "spirits" refers to that which the indwelling spirit gives to us. "The spirits of" in "the spirits of the prophets are subject to the prophets" is a genitive of origin. In other words, it is better to be read as "spirit from". To convey what the Greek grammar intends, the text becomes "the spirits from the prophets are subject to the prophets"

Since there are no definite articles in the Greek of this text at all, the text more faithfully stated is "spirits from prophets are subject to prophets".

In everyday language, this would read "utterances from prophets are subject to prophets".

Paul wanted us to know that those sounds spoken as prophecy, tongues or interpretation are subject to the speaker. The administration of these utterances is my service to discharge and in verse 37, Paul shows that I get better with detailed and accurate knowledge. I can stop, start, repeat, slow down or go faster as occasion demands.

Why did Paul teach the Corinthians that "the spirits of the prophets are subject to the prophets"?

He taught it to them to remind them they were serving others with these spiritual gifts. That knowledge would clarify their thoughts, which in turn shows up in an improved administration of the things of the spirit.

The difference in the excellence of administration between a prophet or knowledgeable saint and an ignorant saint is that while one is given to the careful application of knowledge, the other is not. The prophet or knowledgeable saint does not have more indwelling of the spirit than the ignorant saint. The saint whose administration is produced by knowledge can patiently and painstakingly minister to the saints until they are edified.

11. When I was a child, I spake as a child, I understood as a child, I thought as a child: but when I became a man, I put

away childish things.

1 Corinthians 13:11

Why does the child speak or administer the utterance of the spirit as a child? Paul said it is because of the child's understanding. The way the child thinks hinders the extent to which the child can bring profit. So the utterances that the child gives are not maximised.

Why does the man speak or administer the utterance of the spirit as a man? Again, Paul said it is because the man has put away the child's understanding. This is the knowledge that he later refers to as **epiginosko** in 1 Corinthians 14:37. The knowledge of the prophet or spiritual man.

This man uses the knowledge of the commandments of Christ to examine what he says, why he says what he says and how he says it to maximise edification.

LET YOUR WOMEN KEEP QUIET

On the matter of prophesying, Paul had taught the Corinthians:

> 4. Every man praying or prophesying, having **HIS** head covered, dishonoureth his head. 5. But every woman that prayeth or prophesieth with **HER** head uncovered dishonoureth her head: for that is even all one as if she were shaven.
> 1 Corinthians 11:4-5

So, Paul taught the Corinthians that when they were gathered in church, both the men and the women could pray publicly and prophesy publicly.

Who could prophesy in the Corinthians church? The men and women.

Men and women to pray and prophesy

The men and women who are to pray are the same men and women who are to prophesy. Since prophesying is to speak edification to the church (see 1 Corinthians 14:4), then both men and women are to speak edification too.

> 23. If therefore the whole church be come together into one place, and all speak with tongues, and there come in **THOSE THAT ARE** unlearned, or unbelievers, will they not say that ye are mad? 24. But if all prophesy, and there come in one that believeth not, or **ONE** unlearned, he is convinced of all, he is judged of all:
> 1 Corinthians 14:23-24

The correction about a better way to minister was "But if all prophesy". The "all" that were to prophesy was the whole church. Thus, Paul had made the case for the whole church prophesying, both the men and women.

> 26. How is it then, brethren? when ye come together, every one of you hath a psalm, hath a doctrine, hath a tongue, hath a revelation, hath an interpretation. Let all things be done unto edifying.
> 1 Corinthians 14:26

The brethren are men and women, who he had identified as the "whole church" that were gathered together in verses 23 and 24. Paul's teaching is that when the men and woman come together, everyone has a psalm, a doctrine, a tongue, a revelation, and an interpretation.

Paul's command was "let all things be done unto edifying".

> 12. Even so ye, forasmuch as ye are zealous of spiritual

GIFTS, seek that ye may excel to the edifying of the church.
1 Corinthians 14:12

The old English word "ye" in "even so ye" and in "forasmuch as ye are zealous of spiritual gifts" is a plural pronoun. It means "all of you". So who did Paul address these words to? Paul is addressing "all of you", irrespective of gender.

The word translated zealous in "zealous of spiritual gifts" means to defend, contend for, to desire, or uphold a thing.

> **As students of the apostles, our question should be "does it edify?" or "is this spoken to the right audience" and not "was it a woman who said it or not".**

Who did Paul expect to be zealous of spiritual gifts? Everyone irrespective of gender, should be zealous of or defend, contend for, be desirous of, or uphold spiritual gifts.

The word translated "excel" means to exceed a fixed number of measure, to go above a number, to overflow, to exceed or to have in abundance.

The word translated "seek" in "seek that ye may excel" means to seek after, seek for, aim at, or strive after.

Who did Paul expect to excel to the edifying of the church? Paul teaches that all of you, which means that everyone irrespective of gender, are to exceed a fixed number of measure, go above a number, overflow, or exceed when it comes to edifying of the church.

These are not suggestions. Paul wanted all saints, whether men or women to overflow, or exceed when it comes to edifying of the church. Therefore, we are to read his instructions on utterance in the church in 1 Corinthians 14 from a gender-neutral perspective.

Given that prophesying is the God-given ability in the indwelling spirit and Paul commanded all saints, irrespective of gender to prophesy, all the "he" in 1 Corinthians 14 must not be read to imply male. It is noteworthy that everywhere that you see the words "his", "he" or "him" in 1 Corinthians 14, it is a Greek word better translated as who. In some instances, these pronouns have been added by translators. For example, there is no "him" in 1 Corinthians 14:2. In 1 Corinthians 14:27, the word translated "man" in "if any man speak" means a certain person. Also, in 1 Corinthians 14:37, the "man" in "if any man think himself" means a certain person. The word translated himself in "edifieth himself" (v4) or "speak to himself" (v28) can be translated himself, herself or themselves. We must not read the 1 Corinthians 14 text to confer powers on the male while suspending them for the female. We read as the apostles intended.

> **It is culture and the doctrine of men that condition people to receive more from men than they do women.**

Paul's statements about the exercise of the vocal abilities of the spirit in the assembly are gender-neutral. Wherever the men can speak to the assembly, the women can also speak to the same audience. The distinction is by the spirit and not by gender.

Joel, Peter and Paul agree

Concerning prophesying, Peter had explained:

17. And it shall come to pass in the last days, saith God, I will pour out of my Spirit upon all flesh: and your sons and your daughters shall prophesy, and your young men shall see visions, and your old men shall dream dreams: 18. And on my servants and on my handmaidens I will pour out in those days of my

Spirit; and they shall prophesy:
Acts 2:17-18

Peter got his teaching from Prophet Joel who showed God's plan was "your sons and your daughters shall prophesy". These "your sons and your daughters" would become "my servants" and "my handmaidens". Both Joel and Peter agreed that prophesying was for sons and daughters. Therefore, the power to prophesy is by the spirit and irrespective of gender.

Thus, the ancient prophets knew that all that had the spirit of God were to prophesy irrespective of their gender.

Joel and Peter were not alone in asserting that prophesy was for both sons and daughters. We have shown earlier that Paul agreed with them. Evidently, God's plan of "your sons and your daughters shall prophesy" was fulfilled in the Corinthian church.

What God said, Joel heard and prophesied, Peter explained and Paul taught to the Corinthians who then practiced it – sons and daughters prophesying irrespective of gender.

So why does God use men more to speak to the church?

This is a faulty question which already assumes that God's stance is to use men more. It is culture and the doctrine of men that condition people to receive more from men than they do women.

Did Paul not command the women not to speak to the church?

34. Let your women keep silence in the churches: for it is not permitted unto them to speak; but **THEY ARE COMMANDED** to be under obedience, as also saith the law. 35. And if they will learn any thing, let them ask their

husbands at home: for it is a shame for women to speak in the
church.

1 Corinthians 14:34-35

These words in 1 Corinthians 14:34-35 have perplexed many.

On the ground that 1 Corinthians 14:34-35 do not appear in
the same place in every manuscript of 1 Corinthians and the
fact that the verses contain some vocabulary that is not characteristic of Paul, there are many scholars as well as manuscripts
that say that 1 Corinthians 14:34-35 were added to Paul's text by
others and as such those verses be omitted altogether.

Some bible versions like the NRSV put the whole of verses 34
and 35 in parenthesis. The NRSV has a footnote stating that, in
some ancient manuscripts, verse 34 and 35 are placed after verse
40. By putting these verses in parenthesis, these versions show
that they are not quite clear where to place these verses in order
for them to fit the structure of the whole chapter

Paul's expression, "as also saith the law" cannot be a reference
to the law since these words or similar are not found in the Old
Testament text. If "the Law" means the writings of Moses, the
prophets and the Psalms, we know that the Law does not say
women should be silent, since Joel's prophecy is in the law and it
was Prophet Joel in Joel 2:28, who showed that God's plan was
"your sons and your daughters shall prophesy". In Joel 2:29, Joel
shows that God refers to both "your sons" and "your daughters" as "my servants" and "my handmaidens" respectively. Except we find Joel at variance with Moses, the other prophets and
the Psalms, Joel's prophecy is representative of the teaching of
the law (the holy scriptures from Genesis through Malachi) that
prophesying was for sons and daughters.

Others find that Paul's appeal to the "law" raises the possibility
that Paul was quoting those Corinthians that had written him
and that he was referring to their concepts. Seen in that light, he

might be appealing to some cultural law which the Corinthians had made known to Paul. On a similar note, Paul might be quoting the derogatory views of the Corinthians with the intention of correcting their views that women were to be silent. In such cases, "as saith the law" refers to the extra-biblical customs or traditions of the Corinthians.

Are these words in 1 Corinthians 14:34-35 contrary to other things that Paul had taught clearly elsewhere?

A hasty and traditional reading of verses 34 and 35 makes it look like the things said in those two verses directly opposes what Paul had said in the surrounding text.

Some other scholars see a harmonious flow of thoughts from verses 1 to 33, a gender-based switch in verses 34 and 35, and then from verse 36 onwards the chapter reverted back into the general flow of instruction about utterance which had been the case before verse 34. Therefore, these scholars argue that those two verses talking about women do not fit within the flow of Paul's instruction about the correct administration of utterance.

It is true that if verses 34 and 35 were suppressed, the chapter still reads fluently and its overall lesson about ministering utterance to the saints is easier to catch.

However, this argument that if verses 34 and 35 were suppressed, the chapter still reads fluently, does not have to mean that verses 34 and 35 are errant. Rather, if we are unbiased about Paul's authorship of verses 34 and 35, we should re-investigate verses 34 and 35 anticipating that, just like the other 38 verses, their lesson would also be about ministering utterance to the saints.

Seen in that light, the interpretation of verses 34 and 35 must fit with both the immediate context and the scope of Scripture and the two verses need to be understood and acted upon like the other 38 verses in 1 Corinthians 14.

We have shown that Paul's immediate context was that he commanded all saints, men and women inclusive to overflow when it comes to edifying of the church and that the overall scope of Scripture as evidenced in Joel's prophecy and Peter's explanation was that prophecy was for both sons and daughters.

Keep silence in the churches

> 34. Let your women keep silence in the churches: for it
> is not permitted unto them to speak; but **THEY ARE
> COMMANDED** to be under obedience, as also saith the law.
> 1 Corinthians 14:34

Paul's statement "Let your women keep silence in the churches" shows that his setting is the churches.

Harmonizing the words in verses 34 with Paul's immediate context where he had commanded all saints, men and women inclusive to overflow when it comes to edifying of the church, we ask "where had Paul used that expression "keep silence" earlier?"

> 28. But if there be no interpreter, let him keep silence in the
> church; and let him speak to himself, and to God.
> 1 Corinthians 14:28

The word that has been translated "silent" in "let him keep silent" is **sigao**, a Greek word that means "no sound".

Was this an absolute "no sound" instruction? Was Paul saying that if a person was going to speak in tongues it had to be addressed to the church and that if the audience was not the church, the saint was to utter no sound?

What Paul said was "let him keep silent in the church". That clause at the end is a key one. The "silent" is "in the church".

Since it is constrained by the clause "in the church", this "keep silent" or "no sound" instruction deserves careful consideration. For one, it shows us that the "keep silent" is not absolute. It is "no sound" relative to the church. It does not forbid the saint from uttering any sound under all circumstances.

The man told to "keep silent" was actually commanded "let him speak to himself and to God". So was this man to speak or not? He was to speak to himself and to God. He was just not to speak to the church. "Let him keep silent" is not absolute but relative to the church. This simply means that although the man could speak in tongues in the church, his audience is not the church.

The "and" between "let him keep silence in the church" and "let him speak to himself, and to God" is **kai**, which means that "speak to himself, and to God" is the further explanation of "keep silence in the church". The sentence is better rendered "let him keep silence in the church which is to say let him speak to himself, and to God" (see 1 Corinthians 14:28). Thus, keep silence in the church means to go from the big audience to an audience of you and God. It indicates a change of audience.

In 1 Corinthians 14:28, the word translated "himself" in "let him speak to himself" is a word that means "himself, herself, or themselves". Thus, the 1 Corinthians 14:28 command means that Paul also commands the men as well as the women to "keep silence in the church". This was in order to preserve the edification principle.

Keep silence means to be submitted to the edification principle. It means not to speak to the church but to speak to self and God. Thus, switch audience by speaking to a smaller audience because you are not ready to bring words easy to understand to the larger audience, which is the church.

Paul's "let him keep silence in the church" was actually an instruction to switch audience.

Why was the speaker in tongues told "let him keep silence"? He was told so because the speaker concluded there was no interpreter or no edification. This means the man speaking in tongues did not see himself as the one who should interpret. Rather than the speaker in tongues saying something to the church that the church does not understand, Paul said "let him keep silence" in the church.

Speak prophets speak!

> 28. But if there be no interpreter, let him keep silence in the church; and let him speak to himself, and to God. 29. Let the prophets speak two or three, and let the other judge.
> 1 Corinthians 14:28-29

The mindset in verse 28 is that of the saint whose thought was "I can do tongues but not interpret. Therefore, there is no interpreter".

Paul's instruction in verse 29 corrects the mindset in verse 28.

In verse 29, it is the same Greek word, **laleo** that has been translated "let" and "speak" in "let the prophets speak". **Laleo** means to use words to declare one's mind and disclose one's thoughts. Paul is saying "speak prophets speak". He is emphatic that the prophet is to speak.

While Paul's instruction to the saint in verse 28 is to be silent in the church and exercise tongues as personal devotion to God, he does not tell the prophet to speak to self and to God. The proper thing was for the prophet to speak rather than be silent like the man or woman in verse 28.

The prophet who has spoken in tongues judges by interpreting the tongues to arrive at prophecy, which edifies the church.

Read together, verses 28 and 29 show that it is in the same setting that Paul had commanded one man to keep silence in the church, that he tells another, who he identified as the prophet to speak. The prophet is speaking to the church that which another saint has been silent about in the church.

The Greek word translated "the other" means "the same". Therefore, "let the prophet say and let the other judge", can be rendered "let the prophet say and let the same judge".

In 1 Corinthians 14, "speaking" in the church refers to the ministry of edification to the church. In the light of this edification principle, "let him keep silence in the church" means that the speaker, irrespective of gender, should not speak in the church when his or her words would not bring understanding. The fellow who would speak uninterpreted tongues when he is supposed to minister to the church will not be speaking edification, therefore should be silent "in the church". Thus, keep silence means "recognise you are not ready to minister edification".

What is the judgement in "let the prophets speak two or three, and let the other judge"?

It is the same Greek word **diakrino** that has been translated "judge" and "let" in "let the other judge". It means to "judge", "make a distinction", "determine" or "decide". Paul is saying "judge prophets judge".

The prophet distinguishes himself or herself from the saint who kept silent in the church because of the mental block that says "I can do tongues but not interpret. In context, this prophet's judgment is not to be silent.

Recall that the word that had been translated as "other" in "let the other judge" means "the same". Thus, the prophet that speaks is the same to judge. Paul explains this judgment in verse 31:

> 31. For ye may all prophesy one by one, that all may learn, and all may be comforted.
> 1 Corinthians 14:31

Prophecy is edifying the church with interpreted tongues (see 1 Corinthians 14:5). Thus, to prophesy is to speak tongues and to interpret it for the understanding of the assembly.

Paul's point is that when some saints think that they are to be silent in the church because there is no interpretation (do they expect the interpretation to drop from outer space?), the prophet is the saint who is knowledgeable enough to prophesy or speak tongues and interpret it for the understanding of the assembly. Thus, the judgment in "let the other judge", means that the prophet is expected to be knowledgeable enough to go past that mental block of verse 28 by reasoning "the ability of tongues is the ability of interpretation of tongues".

Where did this judgment come from?

> 37. If any man think himself to be a prophet, or spiritual, let him acknowledge that the things that I write unto you are the commandments of the Lord.
> 1 Corinthians 14:37

Paul mentioned the prophet judging in verse 29 and described him as one who acknowledges. The Greek word translated "acknowledge" is the Greek word **epiginosko**, a word that means a thorough and detailed knowledge. in context, this is the through and comprehensive knowledge of what Paul had written in 1 Corinthians 12, 13, and 14.

Thus, his judgment or decision is from comprehensive knowledge of the epistles. The prophet is the spiritual who uses knowledge to go beyond the mental block that made the man in verse 28 "keep silence in the church". The man kept silence in the church because he had a knowledge gap.

As a student of the word, the prophet will not allow himself stop short of edification of the saints but will co-labour against ignorance by going beyond the silence of verse 28 and speaking edification to the church.

Thus, "let the other judge" means let the prophet speak edification as their decision from the knowledge of God's word, which teaches the saints to go from tongues to understanding for the benefit of the assembly.

The context for "Let your women keep silence"

This is the background knowledge that helps us harmonize verses 34 and 35 with the rest of Paul's instructions in 1 Corinthians 14.

32. And the spirits of the prophets are subject to the prophets. 33. For God is not **THE AUTHOR** of confusion, but of peace, as in all churches of the saints. 34. Let your women keep silence in the churches: for it is not permitted unto them to speak; but **THEY ARE COMMANDED** to be under obedience, as also saith the law. 35. And if they will learn any thing, let them ask their husbands at home: for it is a shame for women to speak in the church.
1 Corinthians 14:32-35

The Greek word for "women" in "let your women keep silence in the churches" is a generic word for a woman of any age or marital status. We will find the specific meaning in the context and setting.

Observe that these women were to ask their husbands at home. Since they had husbands, these were married women. Therefore in 1 Corinthians 14:34-35, Paul was not addressing every woman in the church but only married women – more on this later. Thus, his instructions were not based on gender.

Where were these wives speaking?
They were speaking in the churches of Corinth.

What did Paul say?
Let your women keep silence in the churches. This is more accurately rendered "Let your wives keep silence in the churches".

What was Paul's correction to these wives?
They were to speak the things they had been saying in the churches to their husbands at home.

Why were these wives to be silent in the church but speak at home?

Since it had to be said at home, Paul meant that the audience was the wife and her husband, hence his instruction to "keep silence in the church". These wives were saying to their husbands in the local assembly things that ought to have been reserved for their husbands at home. Therefore, Paul's correction "let your women keep silence in the churches" was his challenge to the elders to train these wives to identify the appropriate audience for the things they were saying.

Since Paul addressed this "Let your women keep silence in the churches" in his correction to the whole church about the administration of utterance and the edification principle, we know that the issue with these wives was one of (in)correct administration of utterance. The wives were using their utterance in the assembly to address their husband about things they should have said at home by husband-wife gist.

The wives would speak in tongues of "angels" (i.e. speak in tongues as one with a message for the assembled saints), only that the understanding in their interpretation of tongues showed that the words of the "interpretation" were a communication of private things meant for their husbands and not to all the saints.

They had spoken in tongues and interpretation, but had not interpreted to edify the assembly. Instead they had followed up their tongues with that which was on their minds for their husbands, which they should have discussed at home.

The implication is: that which is for the home should be kept at home.

Technically, the tongue such wives had spoken was uninterpreted, they had simply voiced their concerns as interpretation.

Home and church contrasted

35. And if they will learn any thing, let them ask their husbands at home: for it is a shame for women to speak in the church.
1 Corinthians 14:35

So, did Paul teach that it is a shame for all women to speak in church?

No, Paul taught no such thing. Rather, he corrected wives who broached domestic matters in the church. The dialogue meant for brother and sister, as husband and wife, is spoken to brother in the presence of all. Paul said "go home, discuss at home".

While Paul had taught in 1 Corinthians 14:5 that except the speaker in tongues interprets there is no edification, and had expanded on that idea in 1 Corinthians 14:9 by explaining what it means to interpret as "except you utter words easy to be understood", in 1 Corinthians 14:34-35, Paul treated a scenario where words have been spoken in tongues after which clear words were given in understanding but the saints were still not edified because what was said in interpretation was not for the church.

There was no interpretation. There was shame.

Basically, Paul had taken the "keep silence in the church" command which he had applied generally to men and women in verse 28 and applies it to married women in verses 34 and 35. They were to separate between domestic matters which were valid when spoken at home and invalid when spoken to the assembly in the church.

This has strong parallels to what he had told these Corinthians in an earlier chapter:

22. What? have ye not houses to eat and to drink in? or despise ye the church of God, and shame them that have not? What shall I say to you? shall I praise you in this? I praise **YOU** not.
1 Corinthians 11:22

He separates between eating and drinking at home and eating when they come together with the brethren.

When the distinction between the private life and the assembly is not understood, those who treat the assembly like their homes are warned "despise ye the church of God, and shame them that have not?".

He continues:

34. And if any man hunger, let him eat at home; that ye come not together unto condemnation. And the rest will I set in order when I come.
1 Corinthians 11:34

They were to satisfy their hunger at home.

When they come in the assembly, it is to share with those who do not have.

When they do in the assembly that which they should have done at home, they come together "unto condemnation", which refers to "shame them that have not" in verse 22. The consequence is that the poor are not taken care of and "for this cause many are weak and sickly among you, and many sleep" (see 1 Corinthians 11:30).

> 33. Wherefore, my brethren, when ye come together to eat, tarry one for another.
> 1 Corinthians 11:33

In the assembly, "tarry one for another".

At home, eat to quench your hunger (see 1 Corinthians 11:34).

Thus, Paul had written about the distinction between the private life and things acceptable in the assembly.

Paul's big point to the Corinthians was for them to distinguish between what was meant for home and what was meant for the assembly.

"Let your women keep silence in the churches" would mean such wives said things not meant for the church setting. They are speaking things that were not edifying the saints present.

A man and wife should be able to talk without resorting to "thus saith the Lord" to pass points across. Such a practice is indecent and out of order. Such wives cannot say "the spirit came upon me and moved me to say it, I couldn't stop the utterance".

The overall concept governing verses 34 and 35 had been stated as "and the spirits of the prophets are subject to the prophets" (see 1 Corinthians 14:32), which means that in the assembly, what the speaker says is subject to the speaker. Therefore, the wives could have waited till they got home.

32. And the spirits of the prophets are subject to the prophets. 33. For God is not **THE AUTHOR** of confusion, but of peace, as in all churches of the saints. 34. Let your women keep silence in the churches: for it is not permitted unto them to speak; but **THEY ARE COMMANDED** to be under obedience, as also saith the law.
1 Corinthians 14:32-34

Again, the word that has been translated "silence" in "Let your women keep silence in the churches" is **sigao**, a Greek word that means no sound, which in 1 Corinthians 14:28 means to be silent in the church while speaking to oneself and God. Thus, in the 1 Corinthians 14 context, silence or **sigao** means no sound to one audience while giving sound to a smaller audience.

Paul did not forbid the sisters from speaking utterance in the churches. Rather his message was to those wives who were using utterance to address domestic issues in the church. His restriction in such cases was that the edification principle made them responsible for watching their utterance and for judging its appropriateness to the church setting. Where the message was inappropriate for the congregation, they were to keep quiet in the church because "the spirits of the prophets are subject to the prophets". They also keep quiet knowing that there is a more appropriate setting at home to say the things they had in mind to their husbands.

Thus, Paul was not addressing every woman in the church but only married women.

"Let them ask their husbands at home" means that the husbands in question were brothers who were present in the meeting with their wives. They were the ones that had been addressed publicly about matters that belong in the home. Thus, Paul was not even addressing every wife in the church but only those wives whose husbands were saints.

Technically, he was addressing those wives whose husbands were present in the assembly and who would have used "interpretation of tongues" to address their husbands on personal matters rather than wait until they got home to discuss as man and wife.

Paul was neither giving an absolute "no sound" instruction to the women in general nor to the wives in particular. He was teaching on distinctions between the home and the church. What edifies in one setting would be inappropriate in the other.

How did Paul conclude the chapter?

> 39. Wherefore, brethren, covet to prophesy, and forbid not to
>   speak with tongues.
>   1 Corinthians 14:39

"Wherefore" means "in conclusion" or "to sum it up".

Observe Paul's closing remarks to the Corinthians after he had corrected the whole assembly about not speaking into the air (verse 9), or speaking as a barbarian (verse 10), commanding both men and women on when to be silent (verse 28) and after he had told the wives not to address private things to the whole church – he said, "brethren, covet to prophesy".

"Brethren" refers to brothers and sisters in the Lord irrespective of gender. Paul identified the administration of prophecy as belonging to the brethren. This is in line with Joel's prophecy and Peter's explanation that your sons and your daughters would prophesy. Since they are saints, all believing men and women have ability by the indwelling spirit of God to edify the church.

In his conclusion, Paul affirms the right of every saint, irrespective of gender to speak edification to the assembly.

The Greek word translated "forbid" in "forbid not to speak with tongues" means "to hinder" or "to deny or refuse one a thing".

Paul's conclusion prevents us from forbidding, hindering, denying or refusing any, including the sisters, from speaking in tongues. Given that speaking in tongues in the assembly is with prophecy in mind, Paul commands not to deny or refuse any, including the sisters, from edifying the saints via prophecy.

All who "covet" in 1 Corinthians 14:39, are the same that "covet earnestly" in 1 Corinthians 12:31, and "desire" in 1 Corinthians 14:1. This is because "covet", "covet earnestly" and "desire" are one Greek word conveying the same point.

We are not to forbid speaking with tongues because speaking in tongues is a valid way to arrive at prophecy. When it comes to the assembly, the saint is not to see speaking in tongues as an end but the door into edifying the saints. We speak in tongues in the assembly in order that we might prophesy.

Since Paul's "let your women keep silence in the churches" was not apostolic prohibition of the sisters from speaking edification to the whole assembly, in the local assembly, we must not limit the effectiveness of our sisters by misunderstanding Paul.

We all covet prophesying unto edification by not forbidding to speak in tongues on the grounds of gender.

As students of the apostles, our question should be "does it edify?" or "is this spoken to the right audience" and not "was it a woman who said it or not".

OTHER BOOKS BY AUTHOR

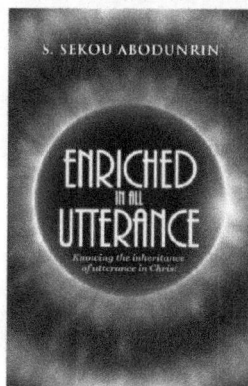

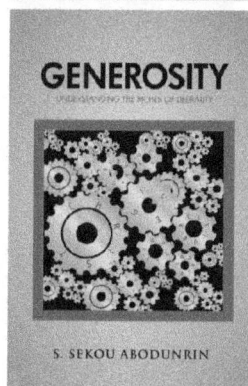

All books available on Amazon

Contact Author

sekou@sekou.me

OTHER BOOKS BY AUTHOR

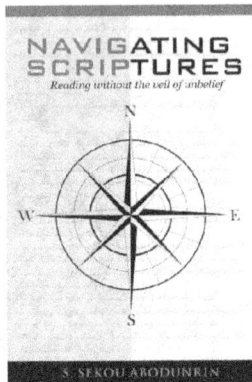

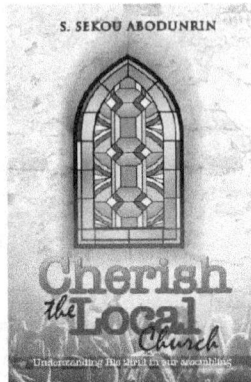

www.ingramcontent.com/pod-product-compliance
Lightning Source LLC
LaVergne TN
LVHW051229080426
835513LV00016B/1491